S0-ADF-132

N 3350 .A6553 1979

Gosudarstvenny i Ermitazh
(Russia)

Western European painting

HOLY SPIRIT LIBRARY

CABRINI COLLEGE, RADNOR, PA.

THE HERMITAGE

LENINGRAD

THE HERMITAGE
PICTURE GALLERY

WESTERN EUROPEAN
PAINTING

AURORA ART PUBLISHERS · LENINGRAD

N
3350
'A6553
1979

6757300

Introduction by
Academician BORIS PIOTROVSKY,
Director General of the Hermitage

Translated from the Russian by
YURY NEMETSKY
Design and layout by
SERGEI DYACHENKO

© AURORA ART PUBLISHERS, LENINGRAD, 1979
Printed and bound in the USSR
Э $\frac{80103\text{-}383}{023(01)\text{-}79}$ без объявления

WESTERN EUROPEAN PAINTING

THE NETHERLANDS

FLANDERS

HOLLAND

SPAIN

ITALY

FRANCE

GERMANY

ENGLAND

THE HISTORY
OF THE GALLERY

The Hermitage, one of the largest and oldest museums in the world, has come a long way from its position as a "place of seclusion" (the French *ermitage*, whence its name) in the palace of the Russian Empress to its present-day standing as an immensely popular national museum. Though in 1778, referring to the Hermitage treasures in a letter to a French correspondent, Catherine II could say: "The only ones to admire all this are the mice and me," and even after it became a "public" museum in 1852 the far from numerous visitors could get admission tickets only from the court office, today the Hermitage is visited annually by over three and a half million people.

At the present time the museum occupies five buildings, each an architectural masterpiece. Four of these are stretched out in a line on the left bank of the Neva in the center of Leningrad: the Winter Palace, built in 1762 by Rastrelli; the Small Hermitage, designed by Vallin de La Mothe in 1769; the Big (or Old) Hermitage, designed by Velten and completed in 1784; and the Hermitage Theatre, built by Quarenghi and linked to the Big Hermitage by an arched bridge over the Winter Canal. The façade of the fifth building, the New Hermitage, built by Stasov and Yefimov in 1851 from a design by Leo von Klenze, fronts Khalturin (formerly Millionnaya) Street, which runs parallel to the Neva. The portico of the New Hermitage is adorned by ten huge figures of atlantes hewn out of granite by Russian craftsmen under the supervision of Terebenev.

The Hermitage today is virtually a museum of the history of culture — from its very dawn, the Stone Age, to modern times. It consists of six major departments which have on display relics of prehistoric culture (for the most part archaeological finds discovered in the territory of the Soviet Union), the culture of antiquity (including treasures coming from excavations of ancient Greek and Roman settlements on the Northern Black Sea coast), the culture of the peoples of the East (beginning with the ancient civilizations of Egypt and Mesopotamia), Russian culture, Western European art (painting, drawing, sculpture and applied art), and numismatics (coins, medals and orders). The entire exposition is housed in 353 rooms. Each year the Hermitage stages no less than twenty temporary exhibitions drawn from its own limitless stocks or loaned by foreign museums.

The Hermitage collection of Western European painting enjoys world renown. Most richly represented are the French, Italian, Flemish and Dutch schools, which were especially popular in Russia in the eighteenth and nineteenth centuries, the period when the collection was being assembled.

Pictures by famous European masters graced the residences of Russian emperors beginning in the early eighteenth century. In 1716, for example, Peter the Great purchased in Amsterdam for his Peterhof palace a number of works by Dutch artists, including Rembrandt's *David's Farewell to Jonathan*. A rich collection of European paintings was housed also in the Catherine Palace erected in 1756 in Tsarskoye Selo (now the town of Pushkin).

ARETINO SPINELLO
St. Benedict

The history of the Hermitage picture gallery begins in the year 1764, when 225 canvases bought a year earlier by Catherine II from the German merchant Johann Ernest Gotzkowsky were delivered to the Winter Palace. This collection consisted for the most part of works by Flemish and Dutch artists and included such famous pieces as Hals's *Portrait of a Young Man Holding a Glove*, Steen's *The Revellers* and Goltzius's *The Baptism of Christ*. This first purchase of pictures was followed by new acquisitions made one after another. Catherine II kept up a regular correspondence with the French encyclopedists Diderot and Grimm, whom she would ask for advice in matters pertaining to the augmentation of her Hermitage collection.

Acting on the Empress's orders, Russian diplomats abroad engaged in the purchase of works of art. In France this assignment fell to the young ambassador Prince Dmitry Golitsyn, a highly educated man, who was to become an honorary member of the St. Petersburg Academy of Sciences. Golitsyn's many personal contacts and his friendship with the progressive-minded public figures and artists of Paris helped him to carry out his mission with success. He was responsible for the purchase in 1766 of such masterpieces as Rembrandt's *The Return of the Prodigal Son* and Poussin's *Tancred and Erminia*. This was followed by the acquisition, also in Paris, of entire collections — Jean de Julienne's, which chiefly included pictures of the Dutch school, in 1767, and Nicolas Gaignat's in 1768. In that same year, also thanks to Golitsyn, the Hermitage acquired for its picture gallery the Hague collection of the Austrian minister Count Cobentzl — forty-six pictures and over four thousand drawings. In 1769, Prince Beloselsky bought for ninety thousand roubles the large Dresden collection of Count Brühl of Saxony. This minister had been entrusted by the Elector of Saxony with the task of selecting pictures for the Dresden Gallery and had simultaneously put together a sizable collection of his own, preferring works of the Flemish and Dutch schools. Among these were such superb pieces as Wouwerman's *View in the Environs of Haarlem* and Mieris's *Oyster Eaters*.

By the end of the 1760s the Hermitage collection of pictures had become too large for the Winter Palace. Additional room for new acquisitions was found in the Small Hermitage, designed by Vallin de la Mothe. This new building consisted of two pavilions (north and south) and a hanging garden between them. Two narrow galleries were added in 1775 by Quarenghi expressly for hanging newly acquired paintings. The north pavilion, which fronts the Neva, was completed in 1769; it had been meant to serve as a "place of seclusion," much like the detached garden pavilions, known as "hermitages," of Tsarskoye Selo and Peterhof (in this case, though, the structure had to be placed in direct propinquity to the palace, not in the garden).

Catherine II used to refer to the entire collection of pictures, antiquities, porcelain and gems located in different parts of the Winter Palace and in the adjacent structures (twenty-three years in the building, from 1764 to 1787) as the Hermitage, and it is by this name that the museum has been known since.

ARETINO SPINELLO
St. Pontien

The acquisition of pictures abroad was not without its mishaps. In 1771, for example, the Brankamp collection, purchased in Genoa, was lost at sea together with the ship carrying it to Russia. This loss was, however, compensated for the very next year when through the good services of Diderot and Tronchin the famous Crozat collection (the Thiers Gallery) was acquired in Paris, in spite of objections from the Parisian public. Crozat's collection included works of different schools selected with sound artistic taste and discretion. Among its masterpieces mention should be made of Giorgione's *Judith*, Raphael's *The Holy Family (Madonna with the Beardless St. Joseph)*, Titian's *Danaë*, Veronese's *The Adoration of the Magi* and *Pietà*, Van Dyck's *Portrait of a Young Man*, Bourdon's *The Death of Dido* and Watteau's *Actors of the Comédie-Française*. Purchased at approximately the same time was the small but very interesting collection owned by the French foreign minister, the Duke of Choiseul.

The provenance of some Hermitage pictures, however, is to this day an unclear point. Between 1764 and 1774 the following masterworks of world art found their way into the Hermitage: *Family Group* by Van Dyck, *Flora* by Rembrandt, *The Marsh* by Ruisdael, *The Dancer La Camargo* by Lancret and *Grace Before Meat* by Chardin.

Some impressions recorded by visitors to the Hermitage in the second half of the eighteenth century have come down to us. Daniel Bernoulli, connected with the St. Petersburg Academy of Sciences, mentions a visit to the Hermitage picture gallery in his Russian travel notes of 1777—78. At that time it occupied the Small Hermitage and the two galleries flanking the hanging garden. Bernoulli was dissatisfied with the way the pictures were hung, "without any order or selection, with different schools intermixed haphazardly," but at the same time remarked that "this collection contains some unexpected treasures, some truly priceless pictures." He also reports that visitors were provided with a catalogue issued in 1774 in sixty copies (this first catalogue listed 2,080 works). Another visitor who complained in his diary of 1776 of the indiscriminate way the pictures were arranged and of the cramped and narrow space in the hanging garden's galleries was the French diplomat Corberon.

The Hermitage pictures were further pressed for space in 1779 with the acquisition in London by Count Musin-Pushkin of the greater part of Sir Robert Walpole's collection from Houghton Hall. This was a sensational purchase, so much so that attempts were made to prevent the collection being taken out of the country. Like Crozat's, Walpole's was a diversified collection and thus a welcome acquisition for the Hermitage because of the long-time preponderance in the museum of Flemish and Dutch paintings. Among the many magnificent canvases that came with the Walpole collection were Rubens's *The Carters* and *The Temple of Janus*, Van Dyck's *Portrait of Elizabeth and Philadelphia Wharton*, Lorrain's *The Bay of Baiae*, Kneller's *Portrait of Grinling Gibbons*, Maratti's *Portrait of Pope Clement IX*, and others.

TINTORETTO
The Nativity of St. John the Baptist

The last major eighteenth-century acquisition was the purchase in 1781 in Paris of 119 pictures, including nine Rembrandts, from the collection of Count Baudouin.

Another development that contributed to the systematic policy of acquisition at that time was the museum's contacts with contemporary European artists; not only were their finished canvases purchased, but new ones commissioned as well. Thus, in 1766 the Hermitage purchased from Greuze his famous canvas *The Paralytic* and in 1785 *The Blacksmith's Shop* from Wright of Derby. Joshua Reynolds, the first President of Britain's Royal Academy, was commissioned by the Russian Imperial Court in 1785 to paint the canvas *The Infant Hercules Strangling the Serpents*, an allegory of the struggle led by the newly emerging Russian state against her enemies; another Reynolds piece, *Cupid Untying the Zone of Venus*, was sold by the artist to the Hermitage in 1786. Most of the orders for pictures were placed with French artists — Van Loo, Chardin and Vigée-Lebrun. Chardin executed for the St. Petersburg Academy of Arts the canvas *Still Life with Attributes of the Arts*, which was brought to Russia by the sculptor Falconet and eventually housed in the Hermitage.

In addition to Imperial collections, the eighteenth century also saw the creation of numerous private collections which boasted some truly superb pieces. Among the best known were the Shuvalov, Beloselsky, Stroganov, Yusupov and Sheremetev collections; many works from these, at one time or another, found their way into the Hermitage or other Soviet museums. Thus, *The Madonna from the Annunciation* by Simone Martini, that gem of early Italian painting, and Filippino Lippi's *The Adoration of the Infant Christ* entered the Hermitage in 1911 from the Stroganov collection.

When Velten completed the Big Hermitage in 1784, its first floor was taken over by the picture gallery, a room-to-room guide to which (with even the number of canvases in each room) is to be found in *A Description of St. Petersburg* published in 1794 by N. Gheorghi. According to the author, there was now more system in the hanging of the pictures which had come to occupy the two galleries along the sides of the hanging garden, the north, so-called La Mothe pavilion, and two suites of rooms in the new building. They were hung so close to each other as to cover the entire surface of the wall; located separately were portraits of members of the Imperial family of the Romanovs and "pictures for copying."

In the same period, two suites of rooms for large-size pictures were added to the south-east corner of the Big Hermitage, as well as a special gallery which was to be a complete reproduction of the world-famous Raphael loggias, painting and all. Catherine II wrote to Grimm in Paris: "I vow to St. Raphael to build a gallery of his loggias, come what may." The copies of

TITIAN
Danaë

FRANCESCO MELZI
Portrait of a Woman

DIEGO VELÁZQUEZ
Portrait of Count Olivares

the frescoes were commissioned to Christopher Unterberger, and the erection of the gallery to Quarenghi, who completed the Hermitage Theatre in 1785. The entire project took ten years to carry out, and it was only in 1788 that the copies were finally mounted. Of course, from our point of view the work of Unterberger and his assistants cannot be termed an exact copy because they freely filled in the missing parts of the original painting, but even so this was definitely a major event in the cultural life of eighteenth-century Russia.

The Hermitage interiors as they were in the late eighteenth century, and as they remained right up to the building of the New Hermitage, have come down to us in sketches made by Julius Friedenreich between 1839 and 1841. His drawings are arid and formal, but undoubtedly factual.

Information on the growth of the picture gallery in the second half of the eighteenth century can also be gleaned from its catalogues. As mentioned above, the first printed catalogue, in French, published in 1774, listed 2,080 canvases. There is a second, manuscript, catalogue in the archives of the Hermitage, which was put out in 1783 and which carries the titles of 2,658 works. By 1797 the number of pictures in all the Imperial palaces reached 3,996. This figure is taken from an inventory drawn up by a special committee appointed after Catherine II's death to determine the number of art works in her Petersburg and suburban residences. Under Paul I some of the Hermitage canvases were moved to the Mikhailovsky (Engineers') Castle in St. Petersburg and to the palaces in Pavlovsk and Gatchina. Later they were all returned to the Hermitage. In the last decade of the eighteenth and in the early nineteenth century there were only occasional acquisitions, some of them true masterpieces, as *The Union of Earth and Water* by Rubens.

At the end of the eighteenth century it became necessary to appoint a custodian. The first man to hold the position was Lucas Pfandzelt. He was succeeded in 1797 by Franz Labensky, who occupied the post for over fifty years. Labensky not only acted as keeper, describing and attributing the pictures, but took an active part in replenishing the gallery's stocks. During a trip to Paris in 1808 he bought the famous Caravaggio canvas *The Lute Player* from the Giustiniani gallery, and in 1810 De Hooch's *A Woman and Her Maid in a Courtyard* from the Parisian antique dealer La Fontaine. Credit for some of the acquisitions must go to the Director of the Louvre Vivant Denon, whose cooperation was fully in keeping with the traditional ties that existed between the Hermitage and the French capital.

At the beginning of the nineteenth century certain alterations were made in the layout of the Hermitage's rooms. The first "statute" of the museum was drawn up whereby it was divided into five departments, second in the list being "the picture gallery, the chamber of rarities, the bronzes and marbles." A restorers' school was set up in the museum where four artists studied the trade under Andrei Mitrokhin, a Labensky appointee (before that the restoration of pictures had been a matter of experimentation, and not always successful at that).

UNKNOWN SPANISH PAINTER.
Active in the second half of
the 15th century
The Entombment

The normal life of the Hermitage was interrupted by the War of 1812. In the September following Napoleon's invasion of Russia the Hermitage was instructed to dispatch all its treasures by "secret expedition." This order was carried out in the strictest secrecy. Only the record books of the court office contain information on the removal of the Hermitage collections and their return in 1813.

Major acquisitions were made after the war. In 1814, the Hermitage purchased 118 pictures from the Malmaison Palace of the Empress Josephine, the first wife of Napoleon. Among them were magnificent works by Flemish, Dutch and French artists, some of which had been seized as booty by Napoleon in other countries. Such works as *The Guard-room* by Teniers, Potter's *The Farm* and Ter Borch's brilliant canvas, *A Glass of Lemonade*, came to the Hermitage with this collection. In 1829, several more pictures of the Malmaison gallery were purchased from Josephine's daughter, Duchess of Saint-Leu.

Another event that led to a significant enlargement of the museum's Spanish section was the purchase in 1814—15 in Amsterdam of a number of pictures from the Coesevelt collection. These included *Portrait of Count Olivares* by Velázquez, *Portrait of Don Diego de Villamayor* by Pantoja de la Cruz and *Still Life* by Pereda. This nucleus was further enriched in 1834 with the entry of several Spanish canvases from the collections of Gessler, the Russian Consul-General in Cádiz, and Paez de la Cadeña, the Spanish ambassador in St. Petersburg.

To commemorate Russia's victory in the War of 1812 a special gallery designed by Carlo Rossi was set aside in the Winter Palace to house portraits of the officers who distinguished themselves in that war, much like the gallery in Windsor Castle with its portraits by Lawrence of those who fought in the battle

BARTOLOMÉ ESTEBAN MURILLO
Boy with a Dog

GEERTGEN TOT SINT JANS (?)
St. Bavo

of Waterloo. The Winter Palace portraits were commissioned to the English painter George Dawe. In all, Dawe and his assistants, the Russian artists Golike and Poliakov, executed 329 portraits of military leaders. Pushkin was among the most ardent admirers of the 1812 War Gallery.

The Hermitage had by then become an important element of Russian culture. Many outstanding artists of the first half of the nineteenth century — Fiodor Tolstoi, Karl Briullov, Alexei Venetsianov, Pavel Fedotov and others — came here to study and copy the works of the Old Masters. However, access to the Imperial museum was still very limited.

In 1837, a great fire destroyed the Winter Palace. It was only at the price of titanic efforts, such as dismantling the passageways and sealing up the door and window apertures with brickwork, that the museum escaped a similar fate. The Winter Palace was rebuilt in a very short space of time, but the reconstruction temporarily diverted the court administration's attention from the Hermitage, which was suffering from an insufficiency of space for its collections: in 1828 the ground floor of the Big Hermitage had been handed over to the State Council and the Committee of Ministers (these premises were reassigned to the museum only in 1855). It now became evident that the construction of a new building for the museum could no longer be postponed.

The edifice was commissioned to Leo von Klenze, the architect who had built the Pinakothek in Munich; the site chosen was the territory between the Winter Canal and the Small Hermitage facing Millionnaya Street plus the courtyards behind the Velten building. Klenze's plan was approved in 1839; the actual construction took about ten years. A special committee, whose leading members were the Russian architects Vasily Stasov and Nikolai Yefimov, was set up to oversee the implementation of the project. The New Hermitage was from the beginning conceived as a museum building whose prime function was to house all the Hermitage collections. The aspect of its halls has been preserved for posterity in the extremely accurate watercolors executed between 1852 and 1860 by Eduard Hau and Lodovico Premazzi.

The pictures were selected and their hanging supervised by a committee chaired by Fiodor Bruni, keeper of the Hermitage gallery since 1849. All canvases were divided into three groups: for display, for transference to other Imperial residences and for sale. As a result 1,219 works were auctioned off. It should be noted that similar sales occur in the history of other European museums — the Dresden Gallery and the Munich Pinakothek. Years later, some of the canvases sold in 1854, Chardin's *Still Life with Attributes of the Arts*, to cite an example, found their way back into the Hermitage.

On the other hand, important acquisitions continued to be made. Several Titians were bought in Venice in 1850, among them two magnificent canvases, *St. Mary Magdalene in Penitence* and *St. Sebastian*. That same year Bruni purchased several pictures at the sale of the collection owned by Willem II of the Neth-

14

JEAN BELLEGAMBE
The Annunciation (triptych)

erlands, among them Guido Reni's *St. Joseph and the Infant Christ*. At a Paris sale in 1852 Bruni bought Zurbarán's *St. Lawrence*, which came from Marshal Soult's collection.

The New Hermitage, proclaimed a "public museum," was opened on February 5, 1852, but a year later the Emperor decreed that "the issue of admission tickets to the Imperial Hermitage and the galleries thereof be entrusted to the court office, not to the keepers of the Hermitage departments." The names of all visitors were to be recorded in a special book.

After the new building of the museum was completed, reconstruction began of the Big Hermitage. The austere interiors created by Quarenghi were redesigned by Stackenschneider as additional palace premises. The reconstruction also took in the La Mothe pavilion, where an impressive but somewhat eclectic hall overlooking the hanging garden was built to replace Catherine's Hermitage.

Twenty-one rooms on the first floor of the New Hermitage were allotted to the picture gallery. The canvases were arranged mainly according to national school, but without any strict system. The last Hermitage catalogue before the transference of the collection to the new building was compiled by Labensky in

15

French in 1838 and contained notes on 1,683 pictures then on display. With the opening of a new exposition the need arose for a new catalogue and a thorough systematization of all the stocks. An inventory completed in 1859 became the main document listing the Hermitage pictures and recording all subsequent acquisitions. Some valuable advice concerning the study of the collection and the layout of the exhibits was offered by Gustav Friedrich Waagen, director of the Berlin Museum's picture gallery, who had been invited for the purpose by the Hermitage authorities. The hanging of the pictures was completed in 1860—61 and by and large remained unchanged up to World War I.

In addition to the spacious halls given over to the works of Rembrandt, Rubens and Van Dyck, and to the extensive collections of national schools (for example, the Dutch in the Tent Hall), pictures were also hung in the modest-size rooms adjoining these halls. Displayed in a separate hall were works by Russian artists, among them Briullov's *The Last Day of Pompeii* and Bruni's *The Brass Serpent*, to name a few. In 1898 all seventy-two pictures of the Russian school were handed over to the Russian Museum.

Though still subordinated to the palace administration, the Hermitage was gradually assuming the character of a *bona fide*

PIETER BRUEGEL I
The Fair

HENDRICK GOLTZIUS
Adam and Eve

FRANS HALS
Portrait of a Man

museum. One of the factors that indubitably contributed to this was the sizable distance separating the exposition from the royal quarters; another was the fact that the personal tastes of the reigning monarch no longer influenced the selection of pictures. In 1863, ninety-nine years after the inauguration of the picture gallery, the first director of the Hermitage was nominated. He was Stepan Gedeonov, head of the Archaeological Commission in Rome prior to his new appointment. Gedeonov greatly eased the restrictions that barred public access to the Hermitage and rescinded the rule whereby only persons in full regimental uniform or tail-coats were admitted to the museum. In 1865, he reported to the palace administration that "steps taken over the past eighteen months to facilitate public access to the Imperial Museum, new acquisitions of important art collections, the issue of catalogues and other like measures had as their consequence an unending flow of visitors to the Hermitage."

The Hermitage came to play a major role in the history of Russian culture. However, many of the barriers hindering free access to the museum were still in force. The art critic Vladimir Stasov (son of the architect who built the New Hermitage) expressed the opinion that the museum was not fulfilling its true function. The Hermitage was deprived of all initiative by its subordination to the court office and by a total lack of funds of its own for the purchase of new pictures. Still, thanks to Gedeonov's untiring energy, Leonardo da Vinci's *Madonna and Child* was purchased in 1866 from the Duke of Litta's gallery in Milan; and in 1870 Raphael's early canvas *Madonna and Child*, painted in 1500 for Count Alfano di Diamante, was acquired in Perugia from Count Conestabile. This masterpiece was at first housed in the Winter Palace, but in 1881 was handed over to the Hermitage picture gallery.

Alexander Vasilchikov, who succeeded Gedeonov as director of the Hermitage, also had difficulties in obtaining funds for the purchase of pictures. Nevertheless, in 1882 he managed to acquire in Florence Fra Beato Angelico's fresco *Madonna and Child with St. Dominic and St. Thomas of Aquinas*, which previously adorned the refectory of the Monastery of San Domenico in Fiesole.

In 1882, the picture collection was enriched by the transfer to the Hermitage of canvases from Peterhof and Gatchina. Among these were Rembrandt's *David's Farewell to Jonathan*, Van Goyen's *Landscape with an Oak*, Van Ostade's *The Scuffle*, Crespi's *In a Cellar*, Bellotto's *New Market Place in Dresden* and Tiepolo's *Maecenas Presenting the Liberal Arts to the Emperor Augustus*. In 1886, seventy-three pictures from the Golitsyn gallery in Moscow, amassed in the second half of the eighteenth century, entered the Hermitage.

The beginning of a serious study of the Hermitage collections is linked with the name of Andrei Somov, keeper of the picture gallery from 1885 to 1909. A prominent art historian and an outstanding connoisseur of painting, he devoted much of his activity to the compiling of *catalogues raisonnés* and to the popularization of the Hermitage treasures, even though the board

ANTHONY VAN DYCK
Self-portrait

GEORGE DAWE
Portrait of Shishkov

of directors was opposed to the idea of using the Hermitage for educational purposes. Somov invited two more art experts, Ernest Liphart and James Schmidt, to work in the museum; these latter were especially successful in matters of attribution. Liphart, for example, proved that *Madonna with a Flower*, which entered the Hermitage in 1914 from the Benois collection, was a Leonardo da Vinci work.

Among the significant acquisitions made prior to World War I, especially worthy of mention is the large collection of Flemish and Dutch paintings put together by the famous Russian geographer and traveler Semionov-Tien-Shansky, which was purchased in 1910 and brought to the Hermitage in 1915. Of primary importance was the Khitrovo collection of English paintings, bequeathed to the Hermitage by its owner. Its most interesting pieces are portraits by such well-known English artist as Gainsborough (*Portrait of the Duchess of Beaufort*), Romney (*Portrait of Mrs. Greer*) and Lawrence (*Portrait of Lady Raglan*).

On the eve of World War I the number of visitors to the museum amounted to almost 180 thousand a year. The Hermitage of that period was brilliantly described by Alexander Benois in his *Guide to the Picture Gallery of the Imperial Hermitage* published in 1910. This was a comprehensive assessment of the collection, although the author pointed out that the museum could not be regarded as a manual of the history of culture: certain schools and epochs were well and in many cases superbly represented, but there were also a number of lacunae. In spite of the rearrangement the exposition still had its drawbacks, and its overall character had not changed much in the sixty years of the museum's existence.

The October Revolution made the Hermitage into a state institution which eventually became a museum of the history of world culture. New departments were set up (in particular the Department of the East), but the picture gallery of Western European art lost none of its significance: in fact, it was greatly expanded by the inclusion not only of nineteenth- but of early twentieth-century works as well. Prior to October 1917 the museum had been an annex, as it were, of the Winter Palace; after the revolution it was the Winter Palace that was, at first partially, later entirely, incorporated into the museum as an outstanding architectural and historic monument.

On October 5, 1918 the Council of People's Commissars issued a decree on the itemization and preservation of historical and artistic monuments. From the very first days of Soviet power Lenin repeatedly pointed out that the creation of a new, socialist, culture could be based only on the achievements of world culture, which in the past belonged to the ruling classes. The preservation of art works of museum value was entrusted to the State Museum Reserve, which had its headquarters in the Winter Palace. This body's function was to assemble works of art and distribute them among the country's museums. As a result, a number of canvases from nationalized private collections entered the Hermitage, filling in many of the gaps in its

KEES VAN DONGEN
Lady in a Black Hat

PABLO PICASSO
Portrait of Soler

stocks, especially as regards nineteenth-century art: *Sappho and Phaon* by David, *Napoleon at Arcole* by Gros, *Portrait of Josephine* by Gérard, *Portrait of Count Guryev* by Ingres, and others. In 1922, the Academy of Arts turned over to the Hermitage the so-called Kushelev gallery, a collection built up by Count Kushelev-Bezborodko in the 1860s and 1870s. This included Jordaens's *Feast of the King of Beans*, Delacroix's *Lion Hunt in Morocco* and *Arab Saddling His Horse*, Troyon's *On the Way to the Market*, Millet's *Peasant Women Carrying Firewood*, Courbet's *Landscape with a Dead Horse* and other superb canvases which enabled the museum to have nineteenth-century Western European painting, a very interesting and important chapter in the history of world art, amply represented in its exposition.

In 1930—31, all the work of the Hermitage was put on a new footing: the museum's pattern of organization was altered, the exposition rearranged so as to stress art's links with history, the picture gallery was provided with additional space in the Winter Palace. A systematic study and detailed itemization of the collections were started. The volume of restoration work cooperation between the Hermitage and the oldest European museums began.

These activities were interrupted by the War of 1941—45. In the very first days of the war the Hermitage collections were taken out of the city and dispatched to Sverdlovsk, deep in the hinterland. The museum staff who traveled with the collections continued their research work even there. Those that stayed behind undertook, under very harsh conditions, the conservation of the remaining collections and of the museum building itself.

In October 1945 all the evacuated treasures were returned to the Hermitage intact and there began the revival and expansion of its exposition, including the picture gallery, which was allotted several more rooms.

The Hermitage collection was significantly enlarged with the transfer to it in 1948 of many canvases from the Moscow Museum of Modern Western Art. The nucleus of this museum had been composed of two famous private collections, chiefly of late nineteenth- and early twentieth-century French painting, built up by Sergei Shchukin and Ivan Morozov (several pictures from the museum had come into the Hermitage in 1930 and 1931). It is this transfer that enriched the Hermitage collection with canvases by Monet, Sisley, Renoir, Pissarro, Degas, Cézanne, Van Gogh, Gauguin, Bonnard, Matisse, Marquet, Derain and Picasso.

In 1958 a two-volume catalogue of Western European painting in the Hermitage was published listing over four thousand canvases (that is, all the pictures on display plus the finest of the reserve stocks). The catalogue was compiled by the eminent Soviet art historian Vladimir Loewinson-Lessing.

In 1964 the Hermitage celebrated its bicentenary. The museum was awarded the Order of Lenin for its contribution to the aesthetic education of the Soviet people.

The staff of the museum continues to do research on the paintings, compile catalogues of pictures of all schools and publish artbooks, scientific papers and guide books. The scope of restoration work has markedly increased, with new methods being used that yield stunning results. For example, an X-ray investigation of the canvas *The Adoration of the Magi*, earlier thought to be a copy of the Rembrandt original in the Göteborg museum (Sweden), revealed the presence of substantial compositional alterations by the author. This allowed the Hermitage canvas to be recognized as the original and the Göteborg piece as a copy done by one of Rembrandt's pupils. X-ray photography likewise revealed that in *Danaë* Rembrandt removed some of the woman's ornaments to enhance the effect of the golden light emanating from the depths of the picture. It was also discovered that Van Dyck's *Portrait of a Man* was painted over a sketch of Cardinal Guido Bentivoglio, that the French artist Lafosse painted his *Hagar in the Desert* on a canvas that carried a finished male portrait by another artist, and that other monarchs were later depicted over the portrait of Louis XIV in the medallion of *The Allegory of Rule* by the Italian painter Solimena.

The removal of old varnish layers presented some well-known paintings in an entirely new light. The color scheme of Giorgione's famous *Judith*, for example, underwent a complete transformation after the removal of a layer of dark varnish laid on by antiquarians, and of later overpaintings.

The growth of the museum's collections is a never-ending process. In the last few years the Hermitage has acquired works by French and Italian artists, for example, Bellange, Drouet, Troyon, Boudin, Dufy, Vlaminck, Matisse, Stazione, and Guttuso. The Flemish and Dutch sections were enriched by the entry of Teniers and Ostade canvases, the German — by the works of Friedrich and Hans Grundig. The collection of Rockwell Kent's pictures, the artist's gift to the Soviet people, laid the beginnings of the Hermitage's collection of American painting. In 1972, the American collector Armand Hammer presented to the Hermitage the *Portrait of the Actress Antonia Zárate* by Goya, a great master until then not represented in the museum. The Hermitage also continues to receive pictures by modern Polish, Hungarian, Rumanian and German artists.

In recent years the Hermitage has hosted many first-class exhibitions of works from the museums of France, Italy, Great Britain, Holland, the USA, Poland, Hungary, Czechoslovakia, Rumania, the German Democratic Republic, Bulgaria, Japan and other countries, thereby acquainting its visitors with a wide range of outstanding works of world art. On the other hand, exhibitions of Hermitage masterworks in many countries of Europe, Asia and America invariably elicit great interest on the part of art lovers and enjoy wide popularity.

Academician Boris Piotrovsky

PLATES

NETHERLANDISH SCHOOL

JAN PROVOOST

ROBERT CAMPIN

HUGO VAN DER GOES

ROGIER VAN DER WEYDEN

LUCAS VAN VALCKENBORCH

LUCAS VAN LEYDEN

JAN GOSSAERT

JAN BRUEGEL

MASTER OF THE FEMALE HALF-LENGTHS

MARINUS VAN REYMERSWAELE

1 JAN PROVOOST
Mary in Glory

2, 3 ROBERT CAMPIN (MASTER OF FLÉMALLE)
The Trinity. The Virgin and Child before the Firescreen.
Diptych

4—6 HUGO VAN DER GOES
The Adoration of the Magi (left).
The Circumcision. The Massacre of the Innocents (right). Triptych

7, 8 ROGIER VAN DER WEYDEN
St. Luke Drawing a Portrait of the Virgin

9 LUCAS VAN VALCKENBORCH
Village Feast

10—12 LUCAS VAN LEYDEN
The Healing of the Blind Man of Jericho. Triptych.
Heralds (left and right)

13, 14 JAN GOSSAERT (MABUSE)
Descent from the Cross

15 JAN BRUEGEL

Street in a Village

16 MASTER OF THE FEMALE HALF-LENGTHS. Active in the first
half of the 16th century
The Virgin and Child

17 MASTER OF THE FEMALE HALF-LENGTHS
The Virgin and Child. Detail

18 MARINUS VAN REYMERSWAELE
The Tax Collectors (?)

NETHERLANDISH SCHOOL
List of Works Reproduced

1 JAN PROVOOST. *Ca.* 1465—1529
Mary in Glory
Oil on canvas, transferred from a panel. 203×151 cm
Acquisitions 1850. Bought in the sale of the collection of
Willem II, King of Netherlands (The Hague). Inv. No. 417

2, 3 ROBERT CAMPIN (MASTER OF FLÉMALLE).
Ca. 1380—1444
*The Trinity. The Virgin and Child before the
Firescreen.* Diptych. 1433—35
Oil on panel. 34.3×24.5 cm
Acquisitions 1845. D. Tatishchev bequest (St. Peters-
burg). Inv. Nos. 442, 443

4—6 HUGO VAN DER GOES. *Ca.* 1440—1482
The Adoration of the Magi. The Circumcision (left). *The
Massacre of the Innocents* (right). Triptych
Oil on canvas, transferred from a panel. 96.3×77.5 cm
(central portion); 96.2×31.7 cm (wings)
Acquisitions 1810. Inv. No. 403

7, 8 ROGIER VAN DER WEYDEN. *Ca.* 1400—1464
St. Luke Drawing a Portrait of the Virgin
Oil on canvas, transferred from a panel. 102×108.5 cm
Inv. No. 419

9 LUCAS VAN VALCKENBORCH. 1530—1597
Village Feast
Oil on panel. 48.5×73.4 cm
Acquisitions 1772. Formerly in the Duke of Choiseul col-
lection (Paris). Inv. No. 396

10—12 LUCAS VAN LEYDEN. 1489/94—1533
The Healing of the Blind Man of Jericho. Triptych.
Heralds (left and right)
Oil on canvas, transferred from a panel. 115.7×150.3 cm
(central portion); 89×33.5 cm (panels with figures of
heralds)
Acquisitions 1772. Formerly in the Crozat collection
(Paris). Inv. No. 407

13, 14 JAN GOSSAERT (MABUSE). *Ca.* 1478—*ca.* 1533
Descent from the Cross. 1521
Oil on canvas, transferred from a panel. 141×106.5 cm
Acquisitions 1850. Bought in the sale of the collection
of Willem II, King of the Netherlands (The Hague).
Inv. No. 413

15 JAN BRUEGEL. 1568—1625
Street in a Village
Oil on copper. 25.5×38 cm
Acquisitions 1769. Formerly in the Brühl collection (Dres-
den). Inv. No. 430

16, 17 MASTER OF THE FEMALE HALF-LENGTHS.
Active in the first half of the 16th century
The Virgin and Child
Oil on panel. 53.2×42.4 cm
Acquisitions 1922. Formerly in the Stroganov Palace
Museum (Petrograd). Inv. No. 4090

18 MARINUS VAN REYMERSWAELE. *Ca.* 1490 —
after 1567
The Tax Collectors (?)
Oil on canvas, transferred from a panel. 84.3×59.6 cm
Acquisitions 1770s. Inv. No. 423

FLEMISH SCHOOL

PETER PAUL RUBENS

ANTHONY VAN DYCK

JACOB JORDAENS

JAN FYT

FRANS SNYDERS

ADRIAEN BROUWER

DAVID TENIERS THE YOUNGER

LOUIS GALLAIT

19 PETER PAUL RUBENS
Portrait of a Lady-in-Waiting to the Infanta Isabella

20 PETER PAUL RUBENS
Statue of Ceres

21 PETER PAUL RUBENS
Perseus and Andromeda

23, 24 PETER PAUL RUBENS
Coronation of Marie de' Medici

25 ANTHONY VAN DYCK
Portrait of a Man

26 ANTHONY VAN DYCK
Portrait of Anne Dalkeith, the Countess of Morton (?),
and Anne Kirke

27 ANTHONY VAN DYCK
Portrait of Elizabeth and Philadelphia Wharton (?)

28 ANTHONY VAN DYCK
Family Group

29 JACOB JORDAENS
Sts. Paul and Barnabas Preaching at Lystra

30 JACOB JORDAENS
Portrait of the Artist with His Parents, Brothers, and Sisters

32 FRANS SNYDERS
Bowl of Fruits on a Red Tablecloth

33   FRANS SNYDERS
Fish Shop

35 DAVID TENIERS THE YOUNGER
View in the Environs of Brussels

38   LOUIS GALLAIT
The Fisherman's Family

19 PETER PAUL RUBENS. 1577—1640
Portrait of a Lady-in-Waiting to the Infanta Isabella.
Ca. 1625
Oil on panel. 64×48 cm
Acquisitions 1772. Formerly in the Crozat collection
(Paris). Inv. No. 478

20 PETER PAUL RUBENS. 1577—1640
Statue of Ceres. Ca. 1615
Oil on panel (cradled). 90.5×65.5 cm
Acquisitions 1768. Formerly in the Cobentzl collection
(Brussels). Inv. No. 504

21, 22 PETER PAUL RUBENS. 1577—1640
Perseus and Andromeda. 1620—21
Oil on canvas, transferred from a panel. 99.5×139 cm
Acquisitions 1769. Formerly in the Brühl collection (Dresden). Inv. No. 461

23, 24 PETER PAUL RUBENS. 1577—1640
Coronation of Marie de' Medici
Oil on panel (cradled). 49×63 cm
Acquisitions 1772. Formerly in the Crozat collection
(Paris). Inv. No. 516

25 ANTHONY VAN DYCK. 1599—1641
Portrait of a Man. Early 1620s
Oil on canvas. 104.8×85.5 cm (the top, bottom and right-hand side of the canvas have been cut off, and the left-hand side has a later addition about 7 cm in width)
Acquisitions 1772. Formerly in the Crozat collection
(Paris). Inv. No. 552

26 ANTHONY VAN DYCK. 1599—1641
Portrait of Anne Dalkeith, the Countess of Morton (?),
and Anne Kirke. Late 1630s
Oil on canvas. 131.5×150.6 cm (the edges of the original canvas have been straightened out)
Acquired between 1763 and 1774. Inv. No. 540

27 ANTHONY VAN DYCK. 1599—1641
Portrait of Elizabeth and Philadelphia Wharton (?).
Second half of the 1630s
Oil on canvas. 162×130 cm
Acquisitions 1779. Formerly in the Walpole collection
(Houghton Hall, Norfolk, England). Inv. No. 533

28 ANTHONY VAN DYCK. 1599—1641
Family Group. Ca. 1621
Oil on canvas. 113×93.5 cm
Acquired before 1774. Formerly in the Lalive de Jully
collection (Paris). Inv. No. 534

29 JACOB JORDAENS. 1593—1678
Sts. Paul and Barnabas Preaching at Lystra. Ca. 1618
Oil on canvas. 151×233 cm
Acquisitions 1769. Formerly in the Brühl collection (Dresden). Inv. No. 491

30 JACOB JORDAENS. 1593—1678
Portrait of the Artist with His Parents, Brothers, and
Sisters. Ca. 1615
Oil on canvas. 175×137.5 cm
Acquisitions 1779. Formerly in the Walpole collection
(Houghton Hall, Norfolk, England). Inv. No. 484

31 JAN FYT. 1611—1661
Still Life with Flowers, Fruit and a Parrot
Oil on canvas. 133.5×172 cm
Signed bottom left: *Joannes Fyt*
Acquisitions 1923. Formerly in the P. Durnovo collection
(Petrograd). Inv. No. 4575

32 FRANS SNYDERS. 1579—1657
Bowl of Fruits on a Red Tablecloth
Oil on canvas, transferred from a panel. 59.6×90.5 cm
Acquired before 1797. Inv. No. 612

33 FRANS SNYDERS. 1579—1657
Fish Shop
Oil on canvas. 209×341 cm
Signed on the barrel: *F. Snyders fecit*
Acquisitions 1772. Formerly in the Crozat collection
(Paris). Inv. No. 606

34 ADRIAEN BROUWER. *Ca.* 1605—1638
Tavern Scene. Ca. 1632
Oil on panel. 25×33.5 cm
Acquisitions 1771. Formerly in the F. Tronchin collection
(Geneva). Inv. No. 643

35 DAVID TENIERS THE YOUNGER. 1610—1690
View in the Environs of Brussels
Oil on canvas, transferred from a panel. 26.7×38 cm
Signed bottom right: *D. Teniers F.*
Acquisitions 1772. Formerly in the Crozat collection
(Paris). Inv. No. 567

36, 37 DAVID TENIERS THE YOUNGER. 1610—1690
The Guard-room
Oil on panel. 69×103 cm
Signed and dated bottom left: *David Teniers F. 1642*
Acquisitions 1815. Formerly in Josephine Beauharnais's
collection (Malmaison, near Paris). Inv. No. 583

38 LOUIS GALLAIT. 1810—1887
The Fisherman's Family
Oil on panel. 39.5×31.5 cm
Signed and dated bottom right: *Luis Gallait. 1848*
Acquisitions 1921. Formerly in the Gorchakov collection
(Petrograd). Inv. No. 5390

DUTCH SCHOOL

REMBRANDT HARMENSZ VAN RIJN

FRANS HALS

PHILIPS WOUWERMAN

JACOB VAN RUISDAEL

BALTHASAR VAN DER AST

WILLEM KALF

GABRIEL METSU

WILLEM CLAESZ HEDA

GERARD TER BORCH

JAN STEEN

PIETER DE HOOCH

ADRIAEN VAN OSTADE

PAULUS POTTER

ADAM PYNACKER

39 REMBRANDT HARMENSZ VAN RIJN
Flora

40 REMBRANDT HARMENSZ VAN RIJN

David's Farewell to Jonathan

41 REMBRANDT HARMENSZ VAN RIJN
Danaë

42, 43 REMBRANDT HARMENSZ VAN RIJN
The Return of the Prodigal Son

44 REMBRANDT HARMENSZ VAN RIJN
Portrait of an Old Man in Red

45   FRANS HALS
Portrait of a Young Man Holding a Glove

46 PHILIPS WOUWERMAN
View in the Environs of Haarlem

47 JACOB VAN RUISDAEL
Stream in a Wood

48 BALTHASAR VAN DER AST
Still Life with Fruit, Flowers, and a Parrot

49 WILLEM KALF
Still Life

50 GABRIEL METSU
Oyster Eaters

51 WILLEM CLAESZ HEDA
Breakfast with Lobster

52, 53 GERARD TER BORCH

A Glass of Lemonade

54 JAN STEEN
The Loafers

55 PIETER DE HOOCH
A Woman and Her Maid in a Courtyard

56   PIETER DE HOOCH
A Woman and Her Maid in a Courtyard. Detail

57 ADRIAEN VAN OSTADE
Talk by the Fireside

58 PAULUS POTTER
The Farm

59 PAULUS POTTER
The Farm. Detail

60 ADAM PYNACKER

A Barge on the River at Sunset

39 REMBRANDT HARMENSZ VAN RIJN. 1606—1669
Flora
Oil on canvas. 125×101 cm
Signed and dated bottom left: *Rembrandt f. 1634*
Acquired between 1770 and 1774. Inv. No. 732

40 REMBRANDT HARMENSZ VAN RIJN. 1606—1669
David's Farewell to Jonathan
Oil on canvas. 73×61.5 cm
Signed and dated bottom center: *Rembrandt f. 1642*
Acquisitions 1882. Bought for Peter the Great in Amsterdam at an auction of Jan van Beuningen's collection and subsequently displayed in the Monplaisir Palace in Peterhof (near St. Petersburg). Inv. No. 713

41 REMBRANDT HARMENSZ VAN RIJN. 1606—1669
Danaë
Oil on canvas. 185×203 cm
Signed and dated bottom left: *Rembrandt. f. 1636*
Acquisitions 1772. Formerly in the Crozat collection (Paris). Inv. No. 723

42, 43 REMBRANDT HARMENSZ VAN RIJN. 1606—1669
The Return of the Prodigal Son. Ca. 1668—69
Oil on canvas (additions 10 cm in width on the right and at the bottom). 262×205 cm
Signed bottom left: *R v Ryn f*
Acquisitions 1766. Formerly in the d'Amézune collection (Paris). Inv. No. 742

44 REMBRANDT HARMENSZ VAN RIJN. 1606—1669
Portrait of an Old Man in Red. Ca. 1652—54
Oil on canvas. 108×86 cm
Acquisitions 1769. Formerly in the Brühl collection (Dresden). Inv. No. 745

45 FRANS HALS. *Ca. 1580—1666*
Portrait of a Young Man Holding a Glove
Oil on canvas. 80×66 cm
Signed with monogram bottom right: *FH*
Acquisitions 1764. Formerly in the Gotzkowsky collection (Berlin). Inv. No. 982

46 PHILIPS WOUWERMAN. 1619—1668
View in the Environs of Haarlem
Oil on canvas. 75×64.5 cm
Signed with monogram bottom left: *PHLSW*
Acquisitions 1769. Formerly in the Brühl collection (Dresden). Inv. No. 853

47 JACOB VAN RUISDAEL. 1628/9—1682
Stream in a Wood. Ca. 1663
Oil on canvas. 104×128 cm
Signed bottom left: *J. van Ruisdael*
Acquisitions 1769. Formerly in the Brühl collection (Dresden). Inv. No. 936

48 BALTHASAR VAN DER AST. 1594—1657
Still Life with Fruit, Flowers, and a Parrot. 1630
Oil on panel. 75×104 cm
Signed bottom left: *B. van der Ast*
Acquisitions 1937. Inv. No. 8472

49 WILLEM KALF. 1622—1693
Still Life. Ca. 1659
Oil on canvas. 105×87.5 cm
Signed bottom left: *W. Kalf*
Acquisitions 1915. Formerly in the P. Semionov-Tien-Shansky collection (Petrograd). Inv. No. 2822

50 GABRIEL METSU. 1629—1667
Oyster Eaters
Oil on panel. 55.5×42 cm
Signed top left: *G Metsu*
Acquisitions 1814. Formerly in Josephine Beauharnais's collection (Malmaison, near Paris). Inv. No. 920

51 WILLEM CLAESZ HEDA. 1594—1680/82
Breakfast with Lobster
Oil on canvas. 118×118 cm
Signed and dated bottom center, on the edge of the tablecloth: *Heda 1648*
Acquisitions 1920. Inv. No. 5606

52, 53 GERARD TER BORCH. 1617—1681
A Glass of Lemonade. 1663—64
Oil on canvas, transferred from a panel. 67×54 cm
Acquisitions 1814. Formerly in Josephine Beauharnais's collection (Malmaison, near Paris). Inv. No. 881

54 JAN STEEN. 1626—1679
The Loafers. Ca. 1660
Oil on panel. 39×30 cm
Signed top right: *J. Steen*
Acquisitions 1764. Formerly in the Gotzkowsky collection (Berlin). Inv. No. 875

55, 56 PIETER DE HOOCH. 1629 — after 1684
A Woman and Her Maid in a Courtyard. Ca. 1660
Oil on canvas. 53×42 cm
Acquisitions 1810. Formerly in the possession of the antique dealer La Fontaine (Paris). Inv. No. 943

57 ADRIAEN VAN OSTADE. 1610—1685
Talk by the Fireside. Ca. 1640
Oil on panel. 39.5×34.5 cm
Signed bottom left: *A. Ostade*
Acquisitions 1781. Formerly in the Baudouin collection (Paris). Inv. No. 902

58, 59 PAULUS POTTER. 1625—1654
The Farm
Oil on panel. 81×115.5 cm (a piece 12 cm in width added at the top)
Signed and dated bottom right: *Paulus Potter, 1649*
Acquisitions 1815. Formerly in Josephine Beauharnais's collection (Malmaison, near Paris). Inv. No. 820

60 ADAM PYNACKER. 1622—1673
A Barge on the River at Sunset
Oil on canvas. 43.5×35.5 cm
Signed bottom left: *A. Pynacker*
Acquisitions 1772. Formerly in the Crozat collection (Paris). Inv. No. 1093

SPANISH SCHOOL

EL GRECO

LUIS DE MORALES

JUAN PANTOJA DE LA CRUZ

FRANCISCO DE ZURBARÁN

JOSÉ DE RIBERA

BARTOLOMÉ GONZÁLEZ Y SERRANO (?)

DIEGO VELÁZQUEZ

ANTONIO PUGA

JUAN BAUTISTA DEL MAINO

BARTOLOMÉ ESTEBAN MURILLO

ANTONIO PEREDA

FRANCISCO JOSÉ DE GOYA Y LUCIENTES

IGNACIO ZULOAGA

61 EL GRECO
Sts. Peter and Paul

62 LUIS DE MORALES
Mater Dolorosa

63 LUIS DE MORALES
Madonna and Child with a Cross-shaped Distaff

64, 65 JUAN PANTOJA DE LA CRUZ
Portrait of Don Diego de Villamayor

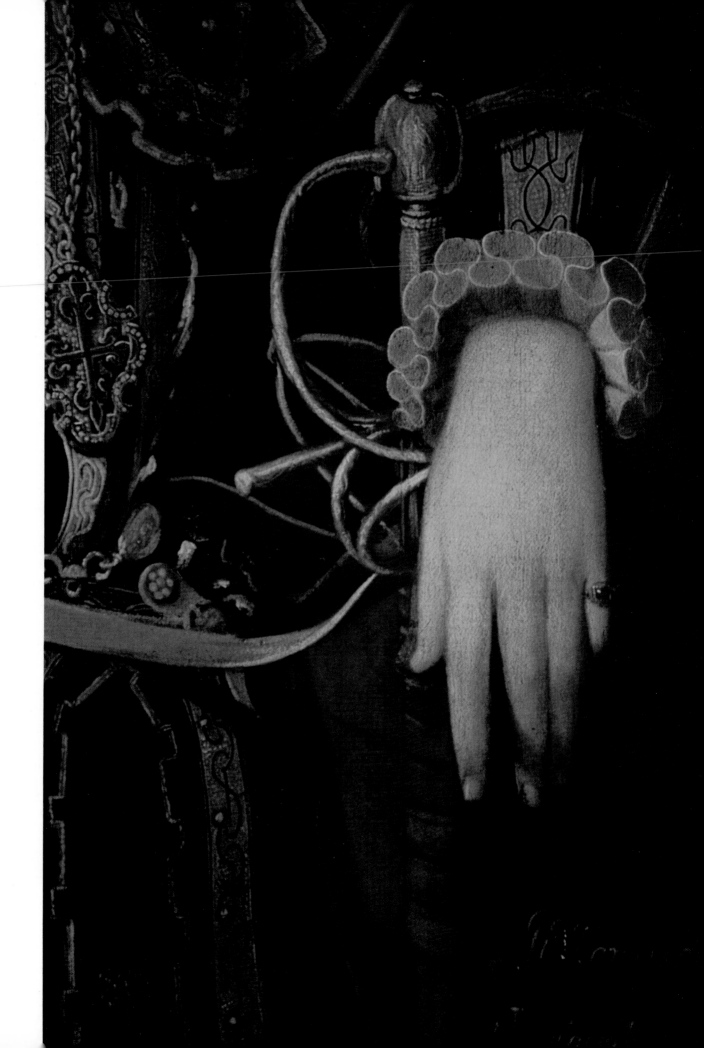

66 FRANCISCO DE ZURBARÁN
The Young Virgin Praying

67 FRANCISCO DE ZURBARÁN
St. Lawrence

68 JOSÉ DE RIBERA

St. Sebastian Nursed by St. Irene

69 BARTOLOMÉ GONZÁLEZ Y SERRANO (?)
Portrait of Margarita Aldobrandini, Duchess of Parma (?)

70, 71 DIEGO VELÁZQUEZ
Luncheon

72 ANTONIO PUGA
The Grinder

73 JUAN BAUTISTA DEL MAINO
The Adoration of the Shepherds

74 BARTOLOMÉ ESTEBAN MURILLO
The Annunciation

75 BARTOLOMÉ ESTEBAN MURILLO
The Immaculate Conception

76 ANTONIO PEREDA
Still Life

77 FRANCISCO GOYA
Portrait of Antonia Zárate

78 IGNACIO ZULOAGA
Gregorio the Dwarf

SPANISH SCHOOL
List of Works Reproduced

61 EL GRECO (DOMENIKOS THEOTOKOPOULOS).
1541—1614
Sts. Peter and Paul. 1587—92
Oil on canvas. 121.5×105 cm
Signed bottom right: *Domenikos Theotokopoulos epoiei*
Acquisitions 1911. Presented by P. Durnovo. Inv. No. 390

62 LUIS DE MORALES. 1520/25—1586 (?)
Mater Dolorosa. 1570s
Oil on panel. 82.5×58 cm
Acquisitions 1814. Formerly in the Coesvelt collection
(Amsterdam). Inv. No. 358

63 LUIS DE MORALES. 1520/25—1586 (?)
Madonna and Child with a Cross-shaped Distaff
Oil on canvas. 71.5×52 cm
Acquisitions 1845. D. Tatishchev bequest (St. Petersburg).
Inv. No. 364

64, 65 JUAN PANTOJA DE LA CRUZ. 1553—1608
Portrait of Don Diego de Villamayor
Oil on canvas. 89×71 cm
Signed and dated bottom right: *Ju*es *Pantoja de la + Fa-*
ciebat 1605 (the last digit, having an old Arabic form,
was incorrectly read as 9 up to 1963)
Inscribed top left: *Didacus de Villamaiore*, right: *Aeta-*
tis suae 17 Anno 1605
Acquisitions 1814. Formerly in the Coesvelt collection
(Amsterdam). In 1833—88 was housed in the Arsenal at
Tsarskoye Selo (near St. Petersburg). Inv. No. 3518

66 FRANCISCO DE ZURBARÁN. 1598—1664
The Young Virgin Praying. Ca. 1660
Oil on canvas. 73.5×53.5 cm
Acquisitions 1814. Formerly in the Coesvelt collection
(Amsterdam). Inv. No. 306

67 FRANCISCO DE ZURBARÁN. 1598—1664
St. Lawrence
Oil on canvas. 292×225 cm
Signed and dated bottom right: *de Zurbaran facie 1636*
Acquisitions 1852. Bought in the Marshal Soult sale
(Paris). Inv. No. 362

68 JOSÉ DE RIBERA. 1591—1652
St. Sebastian Nursed by St. Irene. 1628
Oil on canvas. 156×188 cm
Acquisitions 1829. Bought from the Duchess of Saint-
Leu. Formerly in the Malmaison collection. Inv. No. 325

69 BARTOLOMÉ GONZÁLEZ Y SERRANO (?). 1564—1627
Portrait of Margarita Aldobrandini, Duchess of Parma (?).
1610s
Oil on canvas. 154.5×111.5 cm
Acquisitions 1834. Purchased for the Hermitage in Cadiz
by Gessler, Russian Consul-General in Cádiz. Inv. No.
2721

70, 71 DIEGO VELÁZQUEZ. 1599—1660
Luncheon. 1617—18
Oil on canvas. 108.5×102 cm
Acquired between 1763 and 1774. Inv. No. 389

72 ANTONIO PUGA. Ca. 1602—1648
The Grinder. 1640s
Oil on canvas. 118×158.5 cm
Acquisitions 1814. Formerly in the Coesvelt collection
(Amsterdam). Inv. No. 309

73 JUAN BAUTISTA DEL MAINO. 1578—1641
The Adoration of the Shepherds. Ca. 1613
Oil on canvas. 142.5×101 cm
Signed middle right: *F. Ju. BTA*
Acquisitions 1914. Formerly in the Coesvelt collection
(Amsterdam). Inv. No. 315

74 BARTOLOMÉ ESTEBAN MURILLO. 1617—1682
The Annunciation. 1655—65
Oil on canvas. 142×107.5 cm
Acquisitions 1814. Formerly in the Coesvelt collection
(Amsterdam). Inv. No. 346

75 BARTOLOMÉ ESTEBAN MURILLO. 1617—1682
The Immaculate Conception. 1670—80
Oil on canvas. 196.5×145 cm
Acquisitions 1779. Formerly in the Walpole collection
(Houghton Hall, Norfolk, England). Inv. No. 387

76 ANTONIO PEREDA. 1608—1678
Still Life. 1652
Oil on canvas. 80×94 cm
Acquisitions 1884. Formerly in the Coesvelt collection
(Amsterdam). Inv. No. 327

77 FRANCISCO JOSÉ DE GOYA Y LUCIENTES. 1746—1828
Portrait of Antonia Zárate. 1810 or 1811
Oil on canvas. 71×58 cm
Presented in 1972 by the American art collector Dr. Ar-
mand Hammer. Inv. No. 10198

78 IGNACIO ZULOAGA. 1870—1945
Gregorio the Dwarf. 1908
Oil on canvas. 187×154 cm
Signed bottom left: *I. Zuloaga*
Acquisitions 1934. Formerly in the Museum of Modern
Western Art (Moscow). Inv. No. 7723

ITALIAN SCHOOL

LEONARDO DA VINCI

FRA BEATO ANGELICO DA FIESOLE

FRA FILIPPO LIPPI

CIMA DA CONEGLIANO

RAPHAEL (RAFFAELLO SANTI)

PONTORMO (JACOPO CARUCCI)

ANDREA DEL SARTO

GIORGIONE (GIORGIONE DA CASTELFRANCO)

VERONESE (PAOLO CALIARI)

TITIAN (TIZIANO VECELLIO)

MATTIA PRETI

MICHELANGELO MERISI DA CARAVAGGIO

GUIDO RENI, ANNIBALE CARRACCI

ALESSANDRO TURCHI

DOMENICO FETTI, BERNARDO STROZZI

PIETRO BERRETTINI

CANALETTO (ANTONIO CANALE)

ALESSANDRO MAGNASCO

GIUSEPPE MARIA CRESPI

GIOVANNI BATTISTA TIEPOLO

FRANCESCO GUARDI

POMPEO GIROLAMO BATONI

MASSIMO CAMPIGLI

GIORGIO MORANDI

RENATO GUTTUSO

FILIPPO DE PISIS

79 LEONARDO DA VINCI
Madonna with a Flower (The Benois Madonna)

80 FRA BEATO ANGELICO DA FIESOLE
Madonna and Child with Angels

81   FRA FILIPPO LIPPI
The Vision of St. Augustine

82 CIMA DA CONEGLIANO
The Annunciation

83 RAPHAEL (RAFFAELLO SANTI)
Madonna and Child (The Conestabile Madonna)

84 RAPHAEL (RAFFAELLO SANTI)
The Holy Family (Madonna with the Beardless St. Joseph)

85 PONTORMO (JACOPO CARUCCI)

Madonna and Child with Sts. Joseph and John the Baptist

86 ANDREA DEL SARTO
Madonna and Child with St. Catherine, St. Elizabeth
and St. John the Baptist

87 GIORGIONE (GIORGIONE DA CASTELFRANCO)
Judith

88 GIORGIONE (GIORGIONE DA CASTELFRANCO)
Madonna and Child in a Landscape

89 VERONESE (PAOLO CALIARI)
Pietà

90 TITIAN (TIZIANO VECELLIO)
Flight into Egypt

91 TITIAN (TIZIANO VECELLIO)
St. Sebastian

92 TITIAN (TIZIANO VECELLIO)
St. Mary Magdalene in Penitence

93 MATTIA PRETI
Musical Party

94 MICHELANGELO MERISI DA CARAVAGGIO
The Lute Player

95 GUIDO RENI
Girlhood of the Virgin

97 ALESSANDRO TURCHI
Bacchus and Ariadne

98, 99 DOMENICO FETTI
Portrait of an Actor

100 BERNARDO STROZZI
Allegory of the Arts

101 PIETRO BERRETTINI (PIETRO DA CORTONA)
The Stoning of St. Stephen

103 CANALETTO (ANTONIO CANALE)
The Arrival of the French Ambassador in Venice

104 ALESSANDRO MAGNASCO
Halt of the Brigands

105 GIUSEPPE MARIA CRESPI
In a Cellar

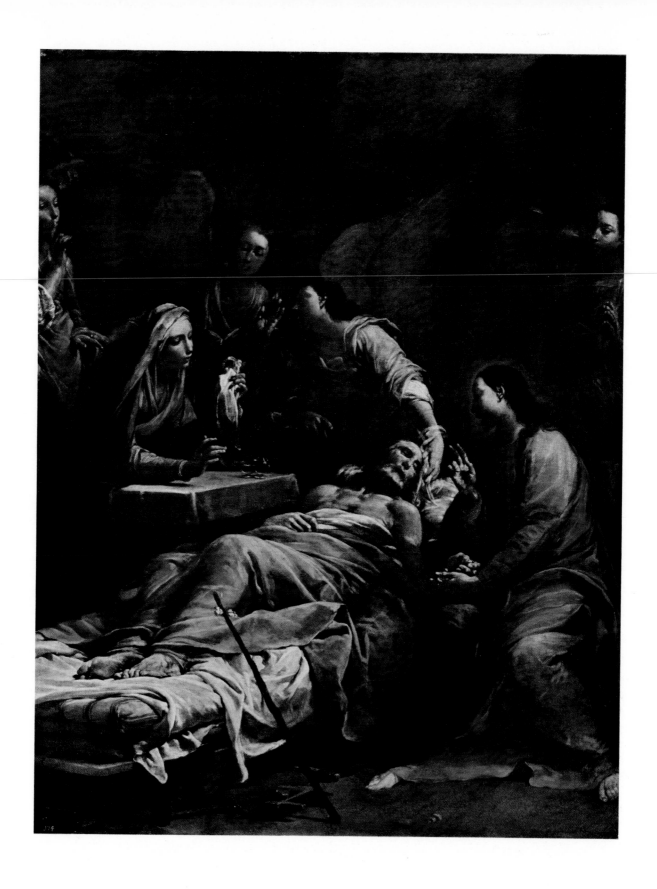

106 GIUSEPPE MARIA CRESPI
Death of St. Joseph

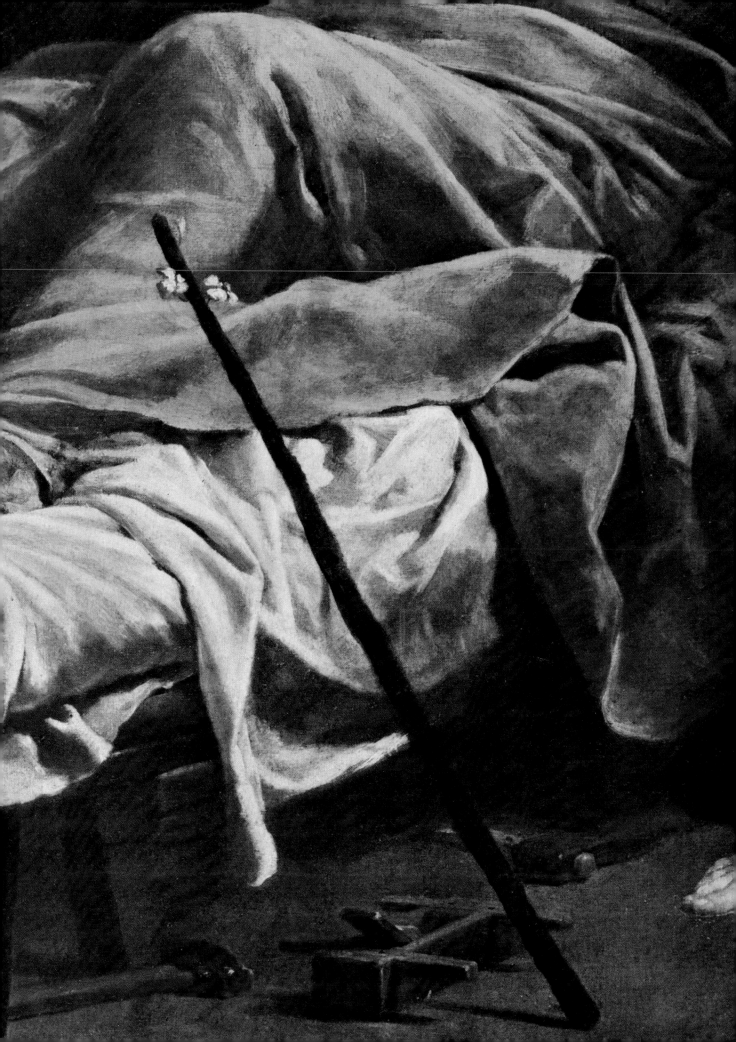

108 GIOVANNI BATTISTA TIEPOLO

Fabius Maximus Quintus in the Senate at Carthage

109 GIOVANNI BATTISTA TIEPOLO
Maecenas Presenting the Liberal Arts to the Emperor Augustus

110 GIOVANNI BATTISTA TIEPOLO
Maecenas Presenting the Liberal Arts to the Emperor Augustus.
Detail

111 FRANCESCO GUARDI
View of a Square with a Palace

112 FRANCESCO GUARDI
Landscape

113 POMPEO GIROLAMO BATONI
Thetis Entrusting Chiron with the Education of Achilles

114 POMPEO GIROLAMO BATONI

Hercules between Love and Wisdom

115 GIORGIO MORANDI
Still Life

116 MASSIMO CAMPIGLI
Seamstresses

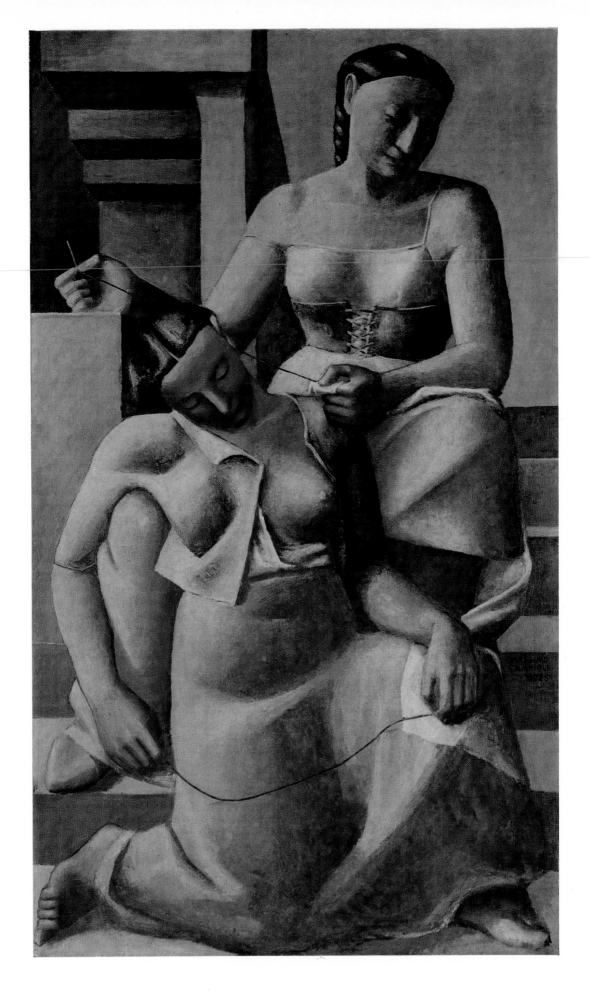

117 RENATO GUTTUSO
The Crowd

118 RENATO GUTTUSO
Rocco and His Son

119 FILIPPO DE PISIS
Flowers

79 LEONARDO DA VINCI. 1452—1519
Madonna with a Flower (The Benois Madonna)
Oil on canvas, transferred from a panel.
49.5×31.5 cm
Acquisitions 1914. Formerly in the M. Benois collection
(Petrograd). Inv. No. 2773

80 FRA BEATO ANGELICO DA FIESOLE. 1387—1455
Madonna and Child with Angels
Tempera on panel. 80×51 cm
Acquisitions 1922. Formerly in the Stroganov Palace Museum (Petrograd). Inv. No. 4115

81 FRA FILIPPO LIPPI. *Ca.* 1406—1469
The Vision of St. Augustine
Tempera and oil on panel. 29×51.5 cm
Acquisitions 1917. Bought from the Princess of Oldenburg (Petrograd). Inv. No. 5511

82 CIMA DA CONEGLIANO. *Ca.* 1459 — *ca.* 1518
The Annunciation
Tempera and oil on canvas, transferred from a panel.
136.5×107 cm
Acquisitions 1886. Formerly in the Golitsyn Museum (Moscow). Inv. No. 256

83 RAPHAEL (RAFFAELLO SANTI). 1483—1520
Madonna and Child (The Conestabile Madonna). 1502—3
Tempera on canvas, transferred from a panel. 17.5×18 cm
Acquisitions 1881. Bought from Count Conestabile della Staffa in 1870 and housed in the Winter Palace (St. Petersburg). Inv. No. 252

84 RAPHAEL (RAFFAELLO SANTI). 1483—1520
The Holy Family (Madonna with the Beardless St. Joseph). 1506
Tempera and oil on canvas, transferred from a panel.
72.5×57 cm
Acquisitions 1772. Formerly in the Crozat collection
(Paris). Inv. No. 91

85 PONTORMO (JACOPO CARUCCI). 1494—1557
Madonna and Child with Sts. Joseph and John the Baptist. 1521—22
Oil on canvas, transferred from a panel. 120×98.5 cm
Acquisitions 1923. Formerly in the collection of Countess E. Mordvinova (Petrograd). Inv. No. 5527

86 ANDREA DEL SARTO. 1486—1531
Madonna and Child with St. Catherine, St. Elizabeth and St. John the Baptist. 1519
Oil on canvas, transferred from a panel. 102×80 cm
Signed on the wheel: *Andrea del Sarto Fiorentino faciebat*
Acquisitions 1814. Formerly in Josephine Beauharnais's collection (Malmaison, near Paris). Inv. No. 62

87 GIORGIONE (GIORGIONE DA CASTELFRANCO).
1478(?)—1510
Judith. Ca. 1504
Oil on canvas, transferred from a panel. 144×66.5 cm
Acquisitions 1772. Formerly in the Crozat collection
(Paris). Inv. No. 95

88 GIORGIONE (GIORGIONE DA CASTELFRANCO).
1478(?)—1510
Madonna and Child in a Landscape. Ca. 1504
Oil on canvas, transferred from a panel. 44×36.5 cm
Acquisitions 1817. Bought in the Creyton sale (St. Petersburg). Inv. No. 185

89 VERONESE (PAOLO CALIARI). 1528—1588
Pietà. Between 1576 and 1582
Oil on canvas. 147×111.5 cm (additions at the left and in the upper part)
Acquisitions 1772. Formerly in the Crozat collection (Paris). Inv. No. 49

90 TITIAN (TIZIANO VECELLIO). 1485/90—1576
Flight into Egypt. Early 1500s
Oil on canvas. 206×336 cm
Acquired between 1763 and 1774. Inv. No. 245

91 TITIAN (TIZIANO VECELLIO). 1485/90—1576
St. Sebastian. 1570s
Oil on canvas. 210×115 cm
Acquisitions 1850. Formerly in the Barbarigo collection (Venice). Inv. No. 191

92 TITIAN (TIZIANO VECELLIO). 1485/90—1576
St. Mary Magdalene in Penitence. 1560s
Oil on canvas. 118×97 cm
Signed on the rock at the left: *Titianvs p.*
Acquisitions 1850. Formerly in the Barbarigo collection (Venice). Inv. No. 117

93 MATTIA PRETI. 1613—1699
Musical Party. Early 1630s
Oil on canvas. 110×147 cm
Acquisitions 1772. Formerly in the Crozat collection (Paris). Inv. No. 1241

94 MICHELANGELO MERISI DA CARAVAGGIO. 1571—1610
The Lute Player. Ca. 1595
Oil on canvas. 94×119 cm
Acquisitions 1808. Bought at the sale of Giustiniani's Roman collection (Paris). Inv. No. 45

95 GUIDO RENI. 1575—1642
Girlhood of the Virgin. 1610s
Oil on canvas. 146×205.5 cm
Acquisitions 1772. Formerly in the Crozat collection (Paris). Inv. No. 198

96 ANNIBALE CARRACCI. 1560—1609
The Three Marys at the Tomb. Ca. 1597
Oil on canvas. 121×145.5 cm
Acquisitions 1836. Formerly in the Coesvelt collection (Amsterdam). Inv. No. 92

97 ALESSANDRO TURCHI. 1578—1649
Bacchus and Ariadne
Oil on canvas. 114.5×147.5 cm
Acquisitions 1782. Purchased from Klostermann, a bookseller in St. Petersburg. Inv. No. 123

98, 99 DOMENICO FETTI. 1589—1623
Portrait of an Actor. 1622—23
Oil on canvas. 105.5×81 cm
Acquisitions 1772. Formerly in the Crozat collection (Paris). Inv. No. 153

100 BERNARDO STROZZI. 1581—1644
Allegory of the Arts. Ca. 1640
Oil on canvas. 152×140 cm
Acquisitions 1930. Formerly in the Stroganov Palace Museum (Leningrad). Inv. No. 6547

101, 102 PIETRO BERRETTINI (PIETRO DA CORTONA).
1596—1669
The Stoning of St. Stephen. Ca. 1660
Oil on canvas. 260.5×149 cm
Acquisitions 1831. Bought in the Godoy sale (Paris). Inv. No. 184

103 CANALETTO (ANTONIO CANALE). 1697—1768
The Arrival of the French Ambassador in Venice. 1740s
Oil on canvas. 181×259.5 cm
Acquired between 1763 and 1774. Inv. No. 175

104 ALESSANDRO MAGNASCO. 1667—1749
Halt of the Brigands. 1710s
Oil on canvas. 112×162 cm
Acquisitions 1922. Formerly in the Museum of the Academy of Arts (Petrograd). Inv. No. 4036

105 GIUSEPPE MARIA CRESPI. 1665—1747
In a Cellar. Ca. 1710
Oil on canvas. 52×42 cm
Acquisitions 1810. Bought in Paris. From 1909 to 1921 was housed in the Peterhof Palace (near St. Petersburg—Petrograd). Inv. No. 225

106, 107 GIUSEPPE MARIA CRESPI. 1665—1747
Death of St. Joseph. Ca. 1712
Oil on canvas. 234.5×187 cm
Acquisitions 1769. Formerly in the Brühl collection (Dresden). Inv. No. 25

108 GIOVANNI BATTISTA TIEPOLO. 1696—1770
Fabius Maximus Quintus in the Senate at Carthage.
1720s
Oil on canvas. 387×224 cm
Acquisitions 1923. Formerly in the Museum of the Stieglitz School of Art and Industry (Petrograd). Inv. No. 7471

109, 110 GIOVANNI BATTISTA TIEPOLO. 1696—1770
Maecenas Presenting the Liberal Arts to the Emperor Augustus. 1743
Oil on canvas. 69.5×89 cm
Acquisitions 1769. Formerly in the Brühl collection (Dresden). Inv. No. 4

111 FRANCESCO GUARDI. 1712—1793
View of a Square with a Palace
Oil on canvas, transferred from a panel. 27×23 cm
Acquisitions 1895. Purchased from V. Kostromitinova (St. Petersburg). Inv. No. 262

112 FRANCESCO GUARDI. 1712—1793
Landscape. Ca. 1790
Oil on canvas. 120×152 cm
Signed bottom right: *Fran^co Guardi F.*
Acquisitions 1928. Formerly in the Gatchina Palace
(near Leningrad). Inv. No. 4305

113 POMPEO GIROLAMO BATONI. 1708—1787
Thetis Entrusting Chiron with the Education of Achilles.
1771
Oil on canvas. 226.5×297.5 cm
Acquisitions 1771. From the second half of the 19th
century housed in the Gatchina Palace (near St. Pe-
tersburg) and in 1926 returned to the Hermitage. Inv.
No. 2608

114 POMPEO GIROLAMO BATONI. 1708—1787
Hercules between Love and Wisdom
Oil on canvas. 245×172 cm
Signed and dated bottom left: *Pompeius Batoni Lucen-
sis, pinxit Romae anno 1765*
Acquisitions 1925. Formerly in the Yusupov Palace Mu-
seum (Leningrad). Inv. No. 4793

115 GIORGIO MORANDI. 1890—1964
Still Life
Oil on canvas. 51×58 cm
Signed top center: *Morandi*
Acquisitions 1948. Formerly in the Museum of Modern
Western Art (Moscow). Inv. No. 8898

116 MASSIMO CAMPIGLI. 1895—1971
Seamstresses
Oil on canvas. 161×97 cm
Signed and dated middle right: *Massimo Campigli 1925*
Acquisitions 1948. Formerly in the Museum of Modern
Western Art (Moscow). Inv. No. 9138

117 RENATO GUTTUSO. Born 1912
The Crowd
Mixed technique. Paper mounted on canvas. 219×347 cm
Acquisitions 1961. Bought from the artist. Inv. No. 10014

118 RENATO GUTTUSO. Born 1912
Rocco and His Son. 1960
Oil on canvas. 145×113 cm
Signed bottom right: *Guttuso*
Acquisitions 1961. Bought from the artist. Inv. No. 10013

119 FILIPPO DE PISIS. 1896—1956
Flowers
Oil on canvas. 65×46 cm
Signed and dated bottom right: *De Pisis 28*
Acquisitions 1948. Formerly in the Museum of Modern
Western Art (Moscow). Inv. No. 9078

FRENCH SCHOOL

CORNEILLE DE LYON (?), THE LE NAIN BROTHERS

NICOLAS POUSSIN, LORRAIN (CLAUDE GELLÉE)

VALENTIN DE BOULLOGNE

JACOB FERDINAND VOET, ANTOINE WATTEAU

JEAN-BAPTISTE SIMÉON CHARDIN

JEAN-HONORÉ FRAGONARD, JACQUES-LOUIS DAVID

PIERRE-PAUL PRUD'HON, CONSTANCE MAYER

FRANÇOIS GÉRARD, JEAN-ANTOINE GROS

JEAN-AUGUSTE DOMINIQUE INGRES

EUGÈNE DELACROIX, HORACE VERNET, JULES DUPRÉ

THÉODORE ROUSSEAU, CAMILLE COROT, CONSTANT TROYON

CHARLES-FRANÇOIS DAUBIGNY, GUSTAVE COURBET

JEAN-FRANÇOIS MILLET, HENRI FANTIN-LATOUR

ERNEST MEISSONNIER, EUGÈNE BOUDIN, ALFRED SISLEY

CLAUDE MONET, PIERRE-AUGUSTE RENOIR, EDGAR DEGAS

CAMILLE PISSARRO, PAUL CÉZANNE

VINCENT VAN GOGH, PAUL GAUGUIN

HENRI EDMOND CROSS (HENRI DELACROIX)

PAUL SIGNAC, HENRI ROUSSEAU, MAURICE DENIS

KER XAVIER ROUSSEL, HENRI CHARLES MANGUIN, PIERRE BONNARD

ALBERT MARQUET, MAURICE DE VLAMINCK, ANDRÉ DERAIN

KEES VAN DONGEN, HENRI MATISSE, PABLO PICASSO

AMÉDÉE OZENFANT, FERNAND LÉGER

120 CORNEILLE DE LYON (?)
Portrait of a Woman

121 THE LE NAIN BROTHERS
A Visit to Grandmother

123 NICOLAS POUSSIN
Landscape with Polyphemus

125 LORRAIN (CLAUDE GELLÉE)
Morning (Landscape with Jacob, Rachel and Leah by the Well)

126 LORRAIN (CLAUDE GELLÉE)
Morning in the Harbor

127 VALENTIN DE BOULLOGNE

Christ Driving the Moneychangers from the Temple

128 JACOB FERDINAND VOET
Portrait of Marie Virginie Borghese-Chigi, Princess Farnese

129, 130 ANTOINE WATTEAU
Savoyard with a Marmot

131 ANTOINE WATTEAU
A Capricious Woman

132 ANTOINE WATTEAU
The Embarrassing Proposal

133 ANTOINE WATTEAU
The Embarrassing Proposal. Detail

134 JEAN-BAPTISTE SIMÉON CHARDIN
Still Life with Attributes of the Arts

135 JEAN-BAPTISTE SIMÉON CHARDIN
Grace Before Meat

137 JACQUES-LOUIS DAVID
Sappho and Phaon

138 JACQUES-LOUIS DAVID
Sappho and Phaon. Detail

139 PIERRE-PAUL PRUD'HON, CONSTANCE MAYER
Innocence Preferring Love to Wealth

140 FRANÇOIS GÉRARD
Portrait of Josephine

141   JEAN-ANTOINE GROS
Napoleon at Arcole

142 JEAN-AUGUSTE DOMINIQUE INGRES
Portrait of Count Guryev

143 EUGÈNE DELACROIX
Arab Saddling His Horse

144 EUGÈNE DELACROIX
Lion Hunt in Morocco

145, 146 HORACE VERNET
Portrait of the Artist

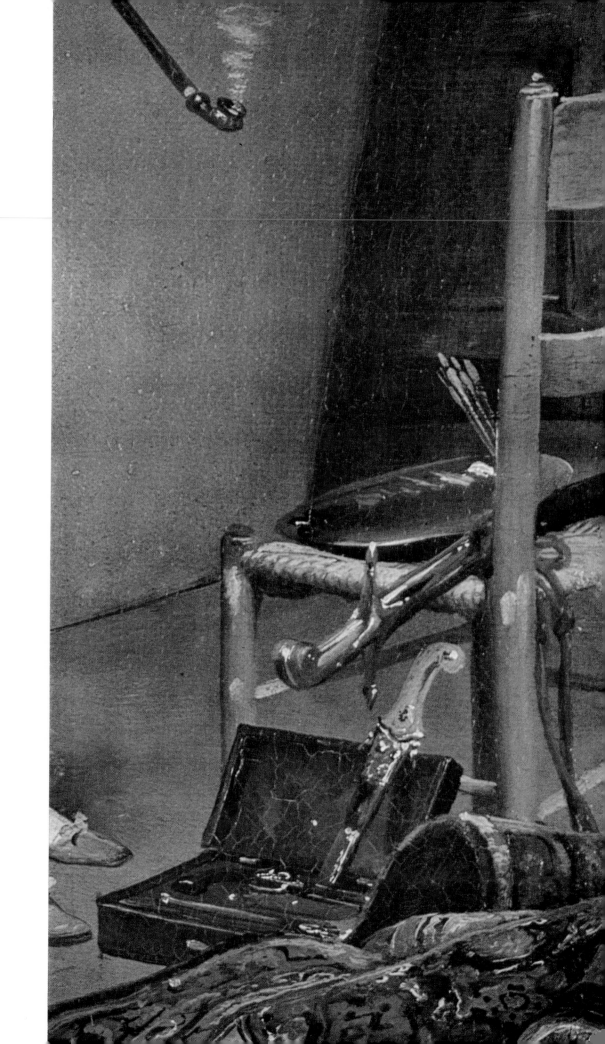

147 JULES DUPRÉ
Autumn Landscape

148 THÉODORE ROUSSEAU
Market Place in Normandy

150 CAMILLE COROT
Peasant Woman Pasturing a Cow on the Skirts of a Wood

151 CAMILLE COROT
Trees in a Marsh

152 CONSTANT TROYON

On the Way to the Market

153 CHARLES-FRANÇOIS DAUBIGNY
The Banks of the Oise

154 GUSTAVE COURBET
Landscape with a Dead Horse

155 JEAN-FRANÇOIS MILLET
Peasant Women Carrying Firewood

156 HENRI FANTIN-LATOUR

Flowers in an Earthenware Vase

157 ERNEST MEISSONNIER

The Musketeer

158 EUGÈNE BOUDIN
The Beach

159 ALFRED SISLEY
River Banks at Saint-Mammès

160 CLAUDE MONET
Lady in a Garden

163 CLAUDE MONET
Waterloo Bridge in London: Fog

164 CLAUDE MONET
Poppy Field

165 PIERRE-AUGUSTE RENOIR
Girl with a Fan

166 PIERRE-AUGUSTE RENOIR
Portrait of the Actress Jeanne Samary

167 PIERRE-AUGUSTE RENOIR
Lady in Black

168 EDGAR DEGAS
After the Bath

170 CAMILLE PISSARRO
Boulevard Montmartre, Paris

171 PAUL CÉZANNE
Girl at the Piano (*Overture to* Tannhäuser)

174 PAUL CÉZANNE
Still Life with Drapery

175 PAUL CÉZANNE
The Smoker

177 PAUL CÉZANNE
Mount Sainte-Victoire

178, 179 VINCENT VAN GOGH
Memory of the Garden at Etten (Ladies of Arles)

180 VINCENT VAN GOGH
The Bush

182 PAUL GAUGUIN
Pastorales Tahitiennes

183 PAUL GAUGUIN
Woman Holding a Fruit

185 HENRI EDMOND CROSS
View of the Church of Santa Maria degli Angeli near Assisi

View of the Church of Santa Maria degli Angeli near Assisi. Detail

187, 188 PAUL SIGNAC
The Marseilles Harbor

190 HENRI ROUSSEAU
In a Tropical Forest

191, 192 MAURICE DENIS
Spring Landscape with Figures (Sacred Grove)

193 HENRI CHARLES MANGUIN
Morning (Woman by the Sea)

194 KER XAVIER ROUSSEL
Village Revels

195 PIERRE BONNARD
Morning in Paris

196   PIERRE BONNARD
Evening in Paris

197 PIERRE BONNARD
The Mediterranean. Triptych

198 ALBERT MARQUET
Rainy Day in Paris (Notre-Dame)

199 ALBERT MARQUET
The Bay of Naples

200 ALBERT MARQUET
The Bay of Naples. Detail

201 MAURICE DE VLAMINCK
View of the Seine

203   ANDRÉ DERAIN
Harbor in Provence (Martigues)

204 ANDRÉ DERAIN

Portrait of an Unknown Man Reading a Newspaper (Chevalier X.)

205 KEES VAN DONGEN
Spring

206 KEES VAN DONGEN
Lucie and Her Partner

208 HENRI MATISSE
The Artist's Family

209 HENRI MATISSE
Conversation

210 HENRI MATISSE
Portrait of the Artist's Wife

211 PABLO PICASSO
The Visit (Two Sisters)

212 PABLO PICASSO
The Absinthe Drinker

213 PABLO PICASSO
The Dance of the Veils

214 PABLO PICASSO
Three Women

215 PABLO PICASSO
Guitar and Violin

216 AMÉDÉE OZENFANT
Still Life: Crockery

217 FERNAND LÉGER
Carte Postale

120 CORNEILLE DE LYON (?). Early 16th century — *ca.* 1575
Portrait of a Woman. 1530s—1540s
Oil on panel. 20×15.5 cm
Acquisitions 1925. Formerly in the Shuvalov Palace Museum (Leningrad). Inv. No. 5697

121 THE LE NAIN BROTHERS. Active first half of the 17th century
A Visit to Grandmother. Late 1640s
Oil on canvas, transferred from the old canvas. 58×73 cm
Acquisitions 1772. Formerly in the Crozat collection (Paris). Inv. No. 1172

122 THE LE NAIN BROTHERS. Active first half of the 17th century
The Dairywoman's Family. 1640s
Oil on canvas. 51×59 cm
Acquired between 1763 and 1774. Inv. No. 1152

123 NICOLAS POUSSIN. 1594—1665
Landscape with Polyphemus. 1649
Oil on canvas. 150×199 cm
Acquisitions 1772. Formerly in the Marquis de Conflans collection (Paris). Inv. No. 1186

124 NICOLAS POUSSIN. 1594—1665
Tancred and Erminia. 1630s
Oil on canvas, transferred from the old canvas. 98.5×146.5 cm
Acquisitions 1766. Bought in the J.-A. Aved sale (Paris). Inv. No. 1189

125 LORRAIN (CLAUDE GELLÉE). 1600—1682
Morning (Landscape with Jacob, Rachel and Leah by the Well)
Oil on canvas. 113×157 cm
Signed and dated bottom right: *Clavdio Lor Romae 1666*
Acquisitions 1814. Formerly in Josephine Beauharnais's collection (Malmaison, near Paris). Inv. No. 1234

126 LORRAIN (CLAUDE GELLÉE). 1600—1682
Morning in the Harbor. Ca. 1649
Oil on canvas. 97.5×120.5 cm
Acquisitions 1779. Formerly in the Walpole collection (Houghton Hall, Norfolk, England). Inv. No. 1243

127 VALENTIN DE BOULLOGNE. 1594—1632
Christ Driving the Moneychangers from the Temple
Oil on canvas. 192×266.5 cm
Acquisitions 1772. Formerly in the Crozat collection (Paris). Inv. No. 1214

128 JACOB FERDINAND VOET. 1639—*ca.* 1700
Portrait of Marie Virginie Borghese-Chigi, Princess Farnese. 1670s
Oil on canvas. 74×57 cm
Acquisitions 1920. Formerly in the Sheremetev Palace Museum (Petrograd). Inv. No. 5712

129, 130 ANTOINE WATTEAU. 1684—1721
Savoyard with a Marmot. 1716
Oil on canvas. 40.5×32.5 cm
Acquired before 1774. Inv. No. 1148

131 ANTOINE WATTEAU. 1684—1721
A Capricious Woman. Ca. 1718
Oil on canvas. 42×34 cm
Acquisitions 1923. Formerly in the Stroganov Palace Museum (Petrograd). Inv. No. 4120

132, 133 ANTOINE WATTEAU. 1684—1721
The Embarrassing Proposal. Ca. 1716
Oil on canvas. 65×84.5 cm
Acquisitions 1769. Formerly in the Brühl collection (Dresden). Inv. No. 1150

134 JEAN-BAPTISTE SIMÉON CHARDIN. 1699—1779
Still Life with Attributes of the Arts
Oil on canvas. 112×140.5 cm
Signed and dated bottom left: *Chardin 1766*
Acquisitions 1766. Inv. No. 5627

135 JEAN-BAPTISTE SIMÉON CHARDIN. 1699—1779
Grace Before Meat
Oil on canvas. 49.5×38.4 cm
Signed and dated in the left background: *Chardin 1744* (the signature at the lower edge of the picture is faked)
Acquired between 1763 and 1774. Inv. No. 1193

136 JEAN-HONORÉ FRAGONARD. 1732—1806
The Lost Forfeit, or the Captured Kiss. 1760s
Oil on canvas. 47×60 cm
Acquisitions 1925. Formerly in the Yusupov Palace Museum (Leningrad). Inv. No. 5646

137, 138 JACQUES-LOUIS DAVID. 1748—1825
Sappho and Phaon
Oil on canvas. 225×262 cm
Signed and dated bottom left: *L. David 1809*
Acquisitions 1925. Formerly in the Yusupov Palace Museum (Leningrad). Inv. No. 5668

139 PIERRE-PAUL PRUD'HON. 1758—1823
CONSTANCE MAYER. 1778—1821
Innocence Preferring Love to Wealth
Oil on canvas. 243×194 cm
Signed and dated bottom left: *Const^ce Mayer. pinxit. 1804*
Acquisitions 1925. Formerly in the Yusupov Palace Museum (Leningrad). Inv. No. 5673

140 FRANÇOIS GÉRARD. 1770—1837
Portrait of Josephine. 1801
Oil on canvas. 178×174 cm
Acquisitions 1919. Formerly in the Leuchtenberg collection (Petrograd). Inv. No. 5674

141 JEAN-ANTOINE GROS. 1771—1835
Napoleon at Arcole
Oil on canvas. 134×104 cm
Acquisitions 1924. Formerly in the Leuchtenberg collection (Petrograd). Inv. No. 5669

142 JEAN-AUGUSTE DOMINIQUE INGRES. 1780—1867
Portrait of Count Guryev
Oil on canvas. 107×86 cm
Signed and dated bottom left: *Ingres Flor 1821*
Acquisitions 1922. Formerly in the Naryshkina collection (Petrograd). Inv. No. 5678

143 EUGÈNE DELACROIX. 1798—1863
Arab Saddling His Horse
Oil on canvas. 56×47 cm
Signed and dated bottom right: *Eug. Delacroix 1855*
Acquisitions 1922. Formerly in the Museum of the Academy of Fine Arts (Petrograd). Inv. No. 3852

144 EUGÈNE DELACROIX. 1798—1863
Lion Hunt in Morocco
Oil on canvas. 74×92 cm
Signed and dated bottom right: *Eug. Delacroix 1854*
Acquisitions 1922. Formerly in the Museum of the Academy of Fine Arts (Petrograd). Inv. No. 3853

145, 146 HORACE VERNET. 1789—1863
Portrait of the Artist
Oil on canvas. 47×39 cm
Signed on the reverse: *Horace Vernet se ipse pinxit. Roma.* Inscribed bottom right: *Souvenir d'amitié d'Horace Vernet au Comte de Fersen. Rome 1835.*
Acquisitions 1919. Formerly in the Fersen collection (Petrograd). Inv. No. 5679

147 JULES DUPRÉ. 1811—1889
Autumn Landscape
Oil on canvas. 51×46 cm
Signed bottom right: *Jules Dupré*
Acquisitions 1922. Formerly in the Museum of the Academy of Fine Arts (Petrograd). Inv. No. 3868

148, 149 THÉODORE ROUSSEAU. 1812—1867
Market Place in Normandy
Oil on panel. 29.5×38 cm
Signed bottom right: *T Rousseau*
Acquisitions 1922. Formerly in the Museum of the Academy of Fine Arts (Petrograd). Inv. No. 3950

150 CAMILLE COROT. 1796—1875
Peasant Woman Pasturing a Cow on the Skirts of a Wood. Ca. 1865—70
Oil on canvas. 47.5×35 cm
Signed bottom right: *Corot*
Acquisitions 1930. Formerly in the Museum of Fine Arts (Moscow). Inv. No. 7166

151 CAMILLE COROT. 1796—1875
Trees in a Marsh. Ca. 1855—60
Oil on canvas. 25.5×38 cm
Signed bottom right: *Corot*
Acquisitions 1922. Formerly in the Somov collection (Petrograd). Inv. No. 5684

152 CONSTANT TROYON. 1810—1865
On the Way to the Market
Oil on canvas. 259×211 cm
Signed and dated bottom left : *C. Troyon 1859*
Acquisitions 1922. Formerly in the Museum of the Academy of Fine Arts (Petrograd). Inv. No. 3966

153 CHARLES-FRANÇOIS DAUBIGNY. 1817—1878
The Banks of the Oise
Oil on canvas. 25.5×41 cm
Signed bottom left: *Ch. Daubigny*
Acquisitions 1919. Inv. No. 3529

154 GUSTAVE COURBET. 1819—1877
Landscape with a Dead Horse. 1850s
Oil on canvas. 45×56 cm
Signed bottom left: *G. Courbet*
Acquisitions 1922. Formerly in the Museum of the Academy of Fine Arts (Petrograd). Inv. No. 3897

155 JEAN-FRANÇOIS MILLET. 1814—1875
Peasant Women Carrying Firewood. Ca. 1858
Oil on canvas. 37.5×29.5 cm
Signed bottom right: *J. F. Millet*
Acquisitions 1922. Formerly in the Museum of the Academy of Fine Arts (Petrograd). Inv. No. 3924

156 HENRI FANTIN-LATOUR. 1836—1904
Flowers in an Earthenware Vase
Oil on canvas. 22.5×29 cm
Signed and dated bottom left: *Fantin 83*
Acquisitions 1946. Inv. No. 8698

157 ERNEST MEISSONNIER. 1815—1891
The Musketeer
Oil on panel. 24×15 cm
Signed and dated bottom right: *E. Meissonier 1870*
Acquisitions 1918. Formerly in the Anichkov Palace
(Petrograd). Inv. No. 5797

158 EUGÈNE BOUDIN. 1824—1898
The Beach
Oil on panel. 23.5×33 cm
Signed bottom left: *E. Boudin*
Acquisitions 1968. Formerly in the Nathan Altman col-
lection (Leningrad). Inv. No. 10028

159 ALFRED SISLEY. 1839—1899
River Banks at Saint-Mammès
Oil on canvas. 50×65 cm
Signed and dated bottom left: *Sisley 84*
Acquisitions 1948. Formerly in the Museum of Modern
Western Art (Moscow). Inv. No. 9167

160 CLAUDE MONET. 1840—1926
Lady in a Garden. 1867
Oil on canvas. 80×99 cm
Signed bottom left: *Claude Monet*
Acquisitions 1930. Formerly in the Museum of Modern
Western Art (Moscow). Inv. No. 6505

161, 162 CLAUDE MONET. 1840—1926
A Haystack
Oil on canvas. 61×81 cm
Signed and dated bottom left: *Claude Monet 86*
Acquisitions 1931. Formerly in the Museum of Modern
Western Art (Moscow). Inv. No. 6563

163 CLAUDE MONET. 1840—1926
Waterloo Bridge in London: Fog
Oil on canvas. 65×100 cm
Signed and dated bottom right: *Claude Monet 1903*
Acquisitions 1930. Formerly in the Museum of Modern
Western Art (Moscow). Inv. No. 6545

164 CLAUDE MONET. 1840—1926
Poppy Field. Ca. 1886—87
Oil on canvas. 59×90 cm
Signed bottom right: *Claude Monet*
Acquisitions 1948. Formerly in the Museum of Modern
Western Art (Moscow). Inv. No. 9004

165 PIERRE-AUGUSTE RENOIR. 1841—1919
Girl with a Fan. 1881
Oil on canvas. 65×50 cm
Signed top right: *Renoir*
Acquisitions 1930. Formerly in the Museum of Modern
Western Art (Moscow). Inv. No. 6507

166 PIERRE-AUGUSTE RENOIR. 1841—1919
Portrait of the Actress Jeanne Samary
Oil on canvas. 173×103 cm
Signed and dated bottom left: *Renoir 78*
Acquisitions 1948. Formerly in the Museum of Modern
Western Art (Moscow). Inv. No. 9003

167 PIERRE-AUGUSTE RENOIR. 1841—1919
Lady in Black. Ca. 1875—76
Oil on canvas. 63×53 cm
Signed middle right: *A. Renoir*
Acquisitions 1930. Formerly in the Museum of Modern
Western Art (Moscow). Inv. No. 6506

168 EDGAR DEGAS. 1834—1917
After the Bath. Ca. 1895
Pastel and gouache on cardboard. 83×72 cm
Signed top right: *Degas*
Acquisitions 1949. Formerly in the Museum of Modern
Western Art (Moscow). Inv. No. 43787

169 CAMILLE PISSARRO. 1830—1903
Place du Théâtre-Français, Paris
Oil on canvas. 66×82 cm
Signed and dated bottom right: *C. Pissarro 98*
Acquisitions 1930. Formerly in the Museum of Modern
Western Art (Moscow). Inv. No. 6509

170 CAMILLE PISSARRO. 1830—1903
Boulevard Montmartre, Paris
Oil on canvas. 73×92 cm
Signed and dated bottom right: *C. Pissarro 97*
Acquisitions 1948. Formerly in the Museum of Modern
Western Art (Moscow). Inv. No. 9002

171 PAUL CÉZANNE. 1839—1906
Girl at the Piano (Overture to Tannhäuser*). Ca.* 1867—
68
Oil on canvas. 57×92 cm
Acquisitions 1948. Formerly in the Museum of Modern
Western Art (Moscow). Inv. No. 9166

172, 173 PAUL CÉZANNE. 1839—1906
Banks of the Marne. 1888
Oil on canvas. 65×81 cm
Acquisitions 1930. Formerly in the Museum of Modern
Western Art (Moscow). Inv. No. 6513

174 PAUL CÉZANNE. 1839—1906
Still Life with Drapery. Ca. 1898—99
Oil on canvas. 53×72 cm
Acquisitions 1930. Formerly in the Museum of Modern
Western Art (Moscow). Inv. No. 6514

175 PAUL CÉZANNE. 1839—1906
The Smoker. Ca. 1889—90
Oil on canvas. 91×72 cm
Acquisitions 1931. Formerly in the Museum of Modern
Western Art (Moscow). Inv. No. 6561

176 PAUL CÉZANNE. 1839—1906
Big Pine near Aix. Ca. 1897—98
Oil on canvas. 72×91 cm
Acquisitions 1948. Formerly in the Museum of Modern
Western Art (Moscow). Inv. No. 8963

177 PAUL CÉZANNE. 1839—1906
Mount Sainte-Victoire. Ca. 1900
Oil on canvas. 78×99 cm
Acquisitions 1948. Formerly in the Museum of Modern
Western Art (Moscow). Inv. No. 8991

178, 179 VINCENT VAN GOGH. 1853—1890
Memory of the Garden at Etten (Ladies of Arles). 1888
Oil on canvas. 74×93 cm
Acquisitions 1948. Formerly in the Museum of Modern
Western Art (Moscow). Inv. No. 9116

180 VINCENT VAN GOGH. 1853—1890
The Bush. 1889
Oil on canvas. 73×92 cm
Signed bottom left: *Vincent*
Acquisitions 1930. Formerly in the Museum of Modern
Western Art (Moscow). Inv. No. 6511

181 VINCENT VAN GOGH. 1853—1890
Cottages. 1890
Oil on canvas. 60×73 cm
Acquisitions 1948. Formerly in the Museum of Modern
Western Art (Moscow). Inv. No. 9117

182 PAUL GAUGUIN. 1848—1903
Pastorales Tahitiennes
Oil on canvas. 86×113 cm
Signed and dated bottom right: *Pastorales Tahitiennes
1893 Paul Gauguin*
Acquisitions 1948. Formerly in the Museum of Modern
Western Art (Moscow). Inv. No. 9119

183 PAUL GAUGUIN. 1848—1903
Woman Holding a Fruit
Oil on canvas. 92×73 cm
Signed and dated bottom left: *P. Gauguin. 93 Eu haere
ia oe.*
Acquisitions 1948. Formerly in the Museum of Modern
Western Art (Moscow). Inv. No. 9120

184 PAUL GAUGUIN. 1848—1903
The Idol
Oil on canvas. 73×91 cm
Signed and dated bottom left: *P. Gauguin 98. Rave te
hiti aamu*
Acquisitions 1948. Formerly in the Museum of Modern
Western Art (Moscow). Inv. No. 9121

185, 186 HENRI EDMOND CROSS (HENRI DELACROIX).
1856—1910
*View of the Church of Santa Maria degli Angeli near
Assisi*
Oil on canvas. 74×92 cm
Signed and dated bottom right: *Henry Edmond Cross 09*
Acquisitions 1948. Formerly in the Museum of Modern
Western Art (Moscow). Inv. No. 8891

187, 188 PAUL SIGNAC. 1863—1935
The Marseilles Harbor. Ca. 1907
Oil on canvas. 46×55 cm
Signed bottom left: *P. Signac*
Acquisitions 1930. Formerly in the Museum of Modern
Western Art (Moscow). Inv. No. 6524

189 HENRI ROUSSEAU. 1844—1910
The Chopin Memorial in the Luxembourg Gardens. 1909
Oil on canvas. 38×47 cm
Acquisitions 1934. Formerly in the Museum of Modern
Western Art (Moscow). Inv. No. 7716

190 HENRI ROUSSEAU. 1844—1910
In a Tropical Forest. 1908—9
Oil on canvas. 46×55 cm
Signed and dated bottom left: *Henri Rousseau 1908*
Acquisitions 1930. Formerly in the Museum of Modern
Western Art (Moscow). Inv. No. 6536

191, 192 MAURICE DENIS. 1870—1943
Spring Landscape with Figures (Sacred Grove)
Oil on canvas. 157×179 cm
Signed with monogram and dated left, on the trunk of
the tree: *MAUD 97*
Acquisitions 1948. Formerly in the Museum of Modern
Western Art (Moscow). Inv. No. 9657

193 KER XAVIER ROUSSEL. 1867—1944
Village Revels
Oil on canvas. 166.5×119.5 cm
Signed and dated bottom right: *K. X. Roussel 913*
Acquisitions 1948. Formerly in the Museum of Modern
Western Art (Moscow). Inv. No. 9165

194 HENRI CHARLES MANGUIN. 1874—1949
Morning (Woman by the Sea). 1906
Oil on canvas. 82×65 cm
Signed bottom right: *Manguin*
Acquisitions 1948. Formerly in the Museum of Modern
Western Art (Moscow). Inv. No. 8956

195 PIERRE BONNARD. 1867—1947
Morning in Paris. 1911
Oil on canvas. 76×122 cm
Signed bottom left: *Bonnard*
Acquisitions 1948. Formerly in the Museum of Modern
Western Art (Moscow). Inv. No. 9107

196 PIERRE BONNARD. 1867—1947
Evening in Paris. 1911
Oil on canvas. 76×121 cm
Signed bottom right: *Bonnard*
Acquisitions 1948. Formerly in the Museum of Modern
Western Art (Moscow). Inv. No. 9105

197 PIERRE BONNARD. 1867—1947
The Mediterranean. Triptych
Oil on canvas. 407×152 cm (central portion); 407
×159 cm (wings)
Signed and dated on the right-hand wing, bottom left:
Bonnard 1911
Acquisitions 1948. Formerly in the Museum of Modern
Western Art (Moscow). Inv. Nos. 9663, 9664, 9665

198 ALBERT MARQUET. 1875—1947
Rainy Day in Paris (Notre-Dame). 1910
Oil on canvas. 81×65 cm
Signed bottom right: *Marquet*
Acquisitions 1930. Formerly in the Museum of Modern
Western Art (Moscow). Inv. No. 6526

199, 200 ALBERT MARQUET. 1875—1947
The Bay of Naples. 1909
Oil on canvas. 61.6×80 cm
Signed bottom right: *Marquet*
Acquisitions 1948. Formerly in the Museum of Modern
Western Art (Moscow). Inv. No. 9150

201 MAURICE DE VLAMINCK. 1876—1958
View of the Seine. 1905—6
Oil on canvas. 54×64.5 cm
Signed bottom right: *Vlaminck*
Acquisitions 1948. Formerly in the Museum of Modern
Western Art (Moscow). Inv. No. 9112

202 ANDRÉ DERAIN. 1880—1954
Mountain Road. 1907
Oil on canvas. 80.5×99 cm
Acquisitions 1948. Formerly in the Museum of Modern
Western Art (Moscow). Inv. No. 9126

203 ANDRÉ DERAIN. 1880—1954
Harbor in Provence (Martigues). 1912
Oil on canvas. 140×89 cm
Signed on the reverse: *a. derain*
Acquisitions 1948. Formerly in the Museum of Modern
Western Art (Moscow). Inv. No. 9101

204 ANDRÉ DERAIN. 1880—1954
*Portrait of an Unknown Man Reading a Newspaper
(Chevalier X.).* 1911—14
Oil on canvas. 160.5×96 cm
Signed on the reverse: *a. derain*
Acquisitions 1948. Formerly in the Museum of Modern
Western Art (Moscow). Inv. No. 9128

205 KEES VAN DONGEN. 1877—1968
Spring. Ca. 1908
Oil on canvas. 80×99 cm
Signed bottom center: *Van Dongen*
Acquisitions 1948. Formerly in the Museum of Modern
Western Art (Moscow). Inv. No. 9130

206 KEES VAN DONGEN. 1877—1968
Lucie and Her Partner. 1911
Oil on canvas. 130×97 cm
Signed bottom left: *Van Dongen*
Acquisitions 1948. Formerly in the Museum of Modern
Western Art (Moscow). Inv. No. 9087

207 HENRI MATISSE. 1869—1954
The Red Room (Harmony in Red)
Oil on canvas. 180×220 cm
Signed and dated bottom left: *Henri Matisse 1908*
Acquisitions 1948. Formerly in the Museum of Modern
Western Art (Moscow). Inv. No. 9660

208 HENRI MATISSE. 1869—1954
The Artist's Family
Oil on canvas. 143×194 cm
Signed and dated on the cross-bar of the stretcher:
Henri Matisse 1911
Acquisitions 1948. Formerly in the Museum of Modern
Western Art (Moscow). Inv. No. 8940

209 HENRI MATISSE. 1869—1954
Conversation. 1909
Oil on canvas. 177×217 cm
Acquisitions 1930. Formerly in the Museum of Modern
Western Art (Moscow). Inv. No. 6521

210 HENRI MATISSE. 1869—1954
Portrait of the Artist's Wife. 1913
Oil on canvas. 145×97 cm
Signed bottom right: *Henri Matisse*
Acquisitions 1948. Formerly in the Museum of Modern
Western Art (Moscow). Inv. No. 9156

211 PABLO PICASSO. 1881—1973
The Visit (Two Sisters)
Oil on canvas, mounted on panel. 152×100 cm
Signed and dated top left: *Picasso 1902*
Acquisitions 1948. Formerly in the Museum of Modern
Western Art (Moscow). Inv. No. 9071

212 PABLO PICASSO. 1881—1973
The Absinthe Drinker. 1901
Oil on canvas. 73×54 cm
Signed top right: *Picasso*
Acquisitions 1948. Formerly in the Museum of Modern
Western Art (Moscow). Inv. No. 9045

213 PABLO PICASSO. 1881—1973
The Dance of the Veils. 1907
Oil on canvas. 150×100 cm
Signed on the back: *Picasso*
Acquisitions 1948. Formerly in the Museum of Modern
Western Art (Moscow). Inv. No. 9089

214 PABLO PICASSO. 1881—1973
Three Women. 1908
Oil on canvas. 200×185 cm
Signed on the back: *Picasso*
Acquisitions 1934. Formerly in the Museum of Modern
Western Art (Moscow). Inv. No. 9658

215 PABLO PICASSO. 1881—1973
Guitar and Violin. 1913
Oil on canvas. 65×54 cm
Signed on the back: *Picasso*
Acquisitions 1948. Formerly in the Museum of Modern
Western Art (Moscow). Inv. No. 9048

216 AMÉDÉE OZENFANT. 1886—1966
Still Life: Crockery
Oil on canvas. 72×60 cm
Signed and dated bottom right: *ozenfant mil neuf cent
vingt*
Acquisitions 1948. Formerly in the Museum of Modern
Western Art (Moscow). Inv. No. 9070

217 FERNAND LÉGER. 1881—1955
Carte Postale
Oil on canvas. 92×65 cm
Signed bottom right: *F. Leger*
Acquisitions 1953. Formerly in the Pushkin Museum of
Fine Arts (Moscow). Inv. No. 9726

GERMAN SCHOOL

AMBROSIUS HOLBEIN

HANS WERTINGER

LUCAS CRANACH THE ELDER

CHRISTOPH AMBERGER

GEORG FLEGEL

CHRISTOPH PAUDISS

CASPAR DAVID FRIEDRICH

JOSEPH ANTON KOCH

HANS VON MARÉES

FRANZ XAVIER WINTERHALTER

FRANZ LENBACH

WILHELM LEIBL

MAX LIEBERMANN

HANS GRUNDIG

HEINRICH EHMSEN

HEINRICH CAMPENDONK

218 AMBROSIUS HOLBEIN
Portrait of a Young Man

219 HANS WERTINGER
Village Feast

220 LUCAS CRANACH THE ELDER
The Virgin and Child under the Apple Tree

221 LUCAS CRANACH THE ELDER
Portrait of a Lady

222 CHRISTOPH AMBERGER
Portrait of a Man

223   GEORG FLEGEL
Still Life with Flowers

224 CHRISTOPH PAUDISS
Still Life

226 CASPAR DAVID FRIEDRICH
Moonrise over the Sea

227 CASPAR DAVID FRIEDRICH
On a Sailing Ship

230 JOSEPH ANTON KOCH
Monastery of St. Francis in the Sabini Mountains near Rome

231, 232 HANS VON MARÉES

Courtyard of the Royal Residence in Munich

233 FRANZ XAVIER WINTERHALTER
Portrait of Princess Yusupova

234 FRANZ LENBACH
Portrait of Wilhelm Busch

236 MAX LIEBERMANN
Girl in a Field

238 HEINRICH EHMSEN
The Execution

239 HEINRICH CAMPENDONK
Human and Animals in Nature

GERMAN SCHOOL
List of Works Reproduced

218 AMBROSIUS HOLBEIN. *Ca. 1495 — ca. 1520*
Portrait of a Young Man
Tempera on panel. 44×32.5 cm
Signed with monogram top right: *AHB*
Inscribed in a frame on the column at the left: *Aetatis suae XX/MDXVIII*
Acquired about 1773. Inv. No. 685

219 HANS WERTINGER. *1465/70—1533*
Village Feast. 1525—1530s
Oil on canvas. 22.5×40 cm
Acquisitions 1925. Formerly in the Shuvalov Palace Museum (Leningrad). Inv. No. 5579

220 LUCAS CRANACH THE ELDER. *1472—1553*
The Virgin and Child under the Apple Tree. 1520—24
Oil on canvas, transferred from a panel. 87×59 cm
At the right, a mark in the form of a dragon
Acquisitions 1851. Inv. No. 684

221 LUCAS CRANACH THE ELDER. *1472—1553*
Portrait of a Lady
Oil on canvas. 88.5×58.6 cm
At the left, monogram *LC*, a mark in the form of a dragon, and date *1526*
Acquired before 1797. Inv. No. 683

222 CHRISTOPH AMBERGER. *1500/10—1562*
Portrait of a Man
Oil on panel. 50.5×42.5 cm
Acquisitions 1772. Formerly in the Crozat collection (Paris). Inv. No. 681

223 GEORG FLEGEL. *1566—1638*
Still Life with Flowers
Oil on panel. 52.5×41 cm
Signed middle right: *G. F.*
Acquisitions 1928. Formerly in the Braz collection (Leningrad). Inv. No. 6054

224, 225 CHRISTOPH PAUDISS. *Ca. 1625—1666*
Still Life
Oil on canvas, transferred from a panel. 62×46.5 cm
Signed and dated in the middle foreground: *Cristofer Paudiss 1660*
Acquisitions 1853. Inv. No. 1035

226 CASPAR DAVID FRIEDRICH. *1774—1840*
Moonrise over the Sea. 1821
Oil on canvas. 135×170 cm
Acquisitions 1928. Formerly in the Ropsha Palace (near Leningrad). Inv. No. 6396

227, 228 CASPAR DAVID FRIEDRICH. *1774—1840*
On a Sailing Ship. 1818—19
Oil on canvas. 71×56 cm
Acquisitions 1958. Formerly in the Peterhof Palace (near Leningrad). Inv. No. 9773

229 CASPAR DAVID FRIEDRICH. *1774—1840*
Riesengebirge. 1835
Oil on canvas. 74×103 cm
Acquisitions 1925. Formerly in the Durnovo collection (Leningrad). Inv. No. 4751

230 JOSEPH ANTON KOCH. *1768—1839*
Monastery of St. Francis in the Sabini Mountains near Rome
Oil on panel. 34×46 cm
Signed and dated bottom right: *C Koch in Roma f. 1812*
Acquisitions 1920. Formerly in the Leuchtenberg collection (Petrograd). Inv. No. 5776

231, 232 HANS VON MARÉES. *1837—1887*
Courtyard of the Royal Residence in Munich. 1862—63
Oil on canvas. 242×162 cm
Acquisitions 1924. Inv. No. 5755

233 FRANZ XAVIER WINTERHALTER. *1806—1873*
Portrait of Princess Yusupova
Oil on canvas. 147×104 cm
Signed and dated middle right: *Fr. Winterhalter. Paris. 1858*
Acquisitions 1925. Formerly in the Yusupov Palace (Leningrad). Inv. No. 5816

234 FRANZ LENBACH. *1836—1904*
Portrait of Wilhelm Busch. Late 1870s
Oil on cardboard. 54×48 cm
Acquisitions 1936. Inv. No. 7752

235 WILHELM LEIBL. *1844—1900*
Savoyard Boy Sleeping
Oil on panel. 44×64 cm
Signed and dated bottom right: *W. Leibl Paris 1869*
Acquisitions 1921. Inv. No. 5780

236 MAX LIEBERMANN. *1847—1935*
Girl in a Field. Ca. 1890
Pastel on paper. 54×79 cm
Signed bottom right: *M. Liebermann*
Acquisitions 1935. Formerly in the Museum of Modern Western Art (Moscow). Inv. No. 42322

237 HANS GRUNDIG. *1901—1958*
Summer Lightnings over the Town
Oil on canvas. 76×94 cm
Signed and dated bottom left: *H. Grundig mai 33*
Acquisitions 1959. Presented by Lea Grundig. Inv. No. 9813

238 HEINRICH EHMSEN. *1886—1963*
The Execution
Oil on canvas. 110×135 cm
Signed and dated bottom right: *Ehmsen 1919*
Acquisitions 1948. Formerly in the Museum of Modern Western Art (Moscow). Inv. No. 9088

239 HEINRICH CAMPENDONK. *1889—1957*
Human and Animals in Nature
Oil on canvas. 95×65 cm
Acquisitions 1948. Formerly in the Museum of Modern Western Art (Moscow). Inv. No. 9137

ENGLISH SCHOOL

MARCUS GHEERAERTS I

THOMAS GAINSBOROUGH

JOHN HOPPNER

JOSEPH WRIGHT OF DERBY

GEORGE ROMNEY

JOSHUA REYNOLDS

HENRY RAEBURN

THOMAS LAWRENCE

GEORGE MORLAND

RICHARD PARKES BONINGTON

FRANK WILLIAM BRANGWYN

240 MARCUS GHEERAERTS I
Portrait of Sir Robert Cecil, Later Earl of Salisbury

241 THOMAS GAINSBOROUGH
Portrait of the Duchess of Beaufort (?)

242 JOHN HOPPNER
Portrait of Richard Brinsley Sheridan

243, 244 JOSEPH WRIGHT OF DERBY
The Blacksmith's Shop

245 GEORGE ROMNEY
Portrait of Mrs. Greer

246 JOSHUA REYNOLDS
Cupid Untying the Zone of Venus

247 HENRY RAEBURN
Mrs. Bethune

248 THOMAS LAWRENCE
Portrait of Lady Emily Fitzroy, Later Lady Raglan

249 GEORGE MORLAND
Approaching Storm

250 RICHARD PARKES BONINGTON
Boats at the Coast. Normandy

251 FRANK WILLIAM BRANGWYN
Charity

ENGLISH SCHOOL
List of Works Reproduced

240 MARCUS GHEERAERTS I. 1561(?)—1635/36
Portrait of Sir Robert Cecil, Later Earl of Salisbury
Oil on panel (cradled). 114.5×89 cm
Inscribed in the right background: *Aetatis suae 32, 1595*
Transferred from the State Museum Reserve in 1921.
Inv. No. 7333

241 THOMAS GAINSBOROUGH. 1727—1788
Portrait of the Duchess of Beaufort (?). Late 1770s
Oil on canvas. 76×64 cm
Acquisitions 1916. A. Khitrovo bequest (Petrograd). Inv.
No. 3509

242 JOHN HOPPNER. 1758—1810
Portrait of Richard Brinsley Sheridan
Oil on canvas (relined). 77×64 cm (the bottom has a
later addition 12 cm in width, the right-hand side, 8 cm)
Acquisitions 1916. A. Khitrovo bequest (Petrograd). Inv.
No. 3510

243, 244 JOSEPH WRIGHT OF DERBY. 1734—1797
The Blacksmith's Shop
Oil on canvas. 105×140 cm
Signed and dated on the hammer, bottom right: *J. Wright
Pinx^t. 1773*
Acquisitions 1774—75. Bought from the artist. Inv. No.
1349

245 GEORGE ROMNEY. 1734—1802
Portrait of Mrs. Greer
Oil on canvas. 76×64 cm
Inscribed on the reverse in Indian ink: *Painted by Rom-
ney 1781*
Acquisitions 1916. A. Khitrovo bequest (Petrograd). Inv.
No. 3511

246 JOSHUA REYNOLDS. 1723—1792
Cupid Untying the Zone of Venus. 1788—89
Oil on canvas. 127.5×101 cm
Acquisitions 1792. Formerly in the Prince G. Potiomkin
collection (St. Petersburg). Inv. No. 1320

247 HENRY RAEBURN. 1756—1823
Mrs. Bethune. 1760s
Oil on canvas. 76×64 cm
Acquisitions 1916. A. Khitrovo bequest (Petrograd). Inv.
No. 3512

248 THOMAS LAWRENCE. 1769—1830
*Portrait of Lady Emily Fitzroy, Later Lady Raglan.
Ca. 1815*
Oil on panel. 76×63 cm
Acquisitions 1916. A. Khitrovo bequest (Petrograd). Inv.
No. 1513

249 GEORGE MORLAND. 1763—1804
Approaching Storm
Oil on canvas. 85×117 cm
Signed and dated bottom right: *G. Morland 1791*
Acquisitions 1919. Formerly in the Fersen collection
(Petrograd). Inv. No. 5834.

250 RICHARD PARKES BONINGTON. 1801—1828
Boats at the Coast. Normandy. Ca. 1825
Oil on canvas. 34×46 cm
Acquisitions 1929. Formerly in the Anichkov Palace
(Leningrad). Inv. No. 5844

251 FRANK WILLIAM BRANGWYN. 1867—1956
Charity
Oil on canvas. 94×91 cm
Signed and dated bottom right: *F. B. 90*
Acquisitions 1948. Formerly in the Museum of Modern
Western Art (Moscow). Inv. No. 9091

ЭРМИТАЖ. КАРТИННАЯ ГАЛЕРЕЯ
Западноевропейская живопись XV—XX веков

ИЗДАТЕЛЬСТВО «АВРОРА». ЛЕНИНГРАД. 1979
Изд. № 2559. (18-70)

PRINTED AND BOUND IN THE USSR